Blessed To Believe

Dr. Nina Gardner

Copyright © 2020 by Dr. Nina Gardner

All rights reserved. No part of this book may be used, reproduced, stored in a retrieval system, or transmitted in any form whatsoever — including electronic, photocopy, recording — without prior written permission from the author, except in the case of brief quotations embodied in critical articles or reviews.

All scripture quotations, unless otherwise indicated, are taken from the *Holy Bible, King James Version*. KJV. Public Domain.

Scripture quotations marked NASB are taken from the New American Standard Bible®, Copyright © 1960, 1962, 1963, 1968, 1971, 1972, 1973, 1975, 1977, 1995 by The Lockman Foundation. Used by permission.

FIRST EDITION

ISBN: 978-1-946466-85-3

Library of Congress Control Number: 2020906701

Published by

3741 Linden Ave. SE, Grand Rapids, MI 49548

Printed in the United States of America

Disclaimer: The views and opinions expressed in this book are solely those of the author and other contributors. These views and opinions do not necessarily represent those of Certa Publishing.
Please note that Certa Publishing's publishing style capitalizes certain pronouns in Scripture that refer to the Father, Son, and Holy Spirit, and may differ from some publishers' styles.

DEDICATION

To my Lord and Savior, Jesus Christ who teaches me how to believe, you are worth believing in.

To my Holy Spirit who has been my constant companion in the making of this book, I am eternally grateful for you.

And to my husband, Bobby, thank you for loving and praying for me always.

ENDORSEMENTS

Enrich your life from Dr. Nina's years of Biblical knowledge and seeking after God's heart. She is an anointed woman of God, and so in love with the Lord. Apply the divine revelations in this book and it will change your life.

Jane Haggard, Sunday Down South, WKWX Radio
Savannah, TN

When Dr. Nina reached out to me about this book, something told me this was something I needed to read. *Blessed To Believe* touched so many points that were hurting in my life, many that I didn't even acknowledge to myself. It forced me to confront and weed out a lot of unbeliefs, and half beliefs. I am eternally grateful for Nina following her leadings and sharing this blessing with me.

Professor Bonnie Sher, Arkansas Tech University
Russellville, AR

I have been blessed by God to know the person, Nina Gardner, as a dear friend and comrade in the gospel of the Kingdom. Her latest writing, *Blessed To Believe,* has clearly reflected the depth of her intimate walk with her Lord and Savior Jesus Christ. This book is written to have a practical but profound impact on the body of Christ. In *Blessed To Believe,* you will be challenged to examine your foundation of faith in your God. It will challenge you to look at your thought processes concerning the supernatural power of the grace of God within you. Do you really believe in the Word of God? Are you really walking in now faith? The wisdom and spiritual insights from Dr. Gardner's personal journals will inspire and release you to dare to believe God in the most challenging life experiences! You will learn to govern your thoughts by the Word of Truth and not out of the imagination of your own heart. The anointing of Holy Spirit is upon the pages and will teach you through the lessons of trial and error of humble servanthood. Nina has allowed us to see the untold story of her journey to maturity of faith through the transparency of her love walk with Jesus. This book will take you to higher realms of faith and new dimensions of grace in the Kingdom of God. It is a tool to equip you to be all that God has called you to be.

I want to thank my friend Nina, for her obedience to the call of God and her willingness to pioneer in the things of the Spirit so that others may enjoy the fruit of her labor. *"May the Lord reward your work, and your wages be full from the Lord, the God of Israel. Under whose wings you have come to take refuge"* (Ruth 2:12, NASB).

Apostle Jeannette Connell
Founder of Freedom Outpost Ministries, Troy MO
& Spiritual Cleansing Ministry

TABLE OF CONTENTS

Preface 9
Introduction 13
Privilege of Believing... 15
Becoming a Believer 19
No Slave to Doubt and Unbelief 23
Transforming Your Thoughts 31
Believing from the Heart 35
How Believing Multiplies 39
Jesus' Works of Believing 45
Crossing Over to Believing 51
Knowing God's Thoughts... 63
Commanding Your Thoughts... 71
Reaching Higher... 81
Realms of New Dimensions 89
Stepping Into Freedom 99
Go Higher, Go Deeper.. 105
About the Author 109

Preface

Some years ago, I read, *"Jesus said unto him, If you can believe, all things are possible to him who believes"* (Mark 9:23). The Holy Spirit illuminated that scripture to me like He was saying, "Pay attention." I thought, "Wow! All things? All things are possible?" That was no small seed that was planted in me and since then that scripture continues to illuminate in my spirit time and again.

We have all heard people say, "I do not believe in …" (and I have been guilty of the same). Yet I know that by the eternal principles, we cannot possess what we don't believe. Believing in something when you don't understand it takes an effort because logic, our natural intelligence, automatically steps in. Believing in something that you cannot see is a huge effort because we humans like to see what we're getting. So, when God says He can do the impossible, we truly believe that He can because He is the Creator. At the same time, we doubt in our hearts that it will happen because it hasn't happened yet, and we can't wrap our minds around the impossible. Again, we humans want to see things manifesting before we believe. Yes indeed, believing is *real* work. It is work to believe against all odds.

Honestly, we believe that Jesus is the Son of God and that He came to save us from our sins, that's why we were converted unto salvation in the first place. And amazingly we can believe in heaven though we have not seen it. So why do we wait to see the miracles manifesting before we can believe? Truly I understand you. This work of believing has been a battle for me as well as for anyone else. That's why down through the years I have consciously and intentionally made the choice to believe in what I cannot see. The eternal principle remains that if I can believe it, I can have what I ask.

Many times, I have faced my giants in this arena. Sometimes I have won the battle of believing despite the odds and at other times not. Although I cannot altogether disregard what my human intellect is saying, I cannot let it dictate to me what is mine through the power of believing God. If a situation is bigger than me and I cannot do anything to change it, then it must be for God to do. So I shift from thinking logically, by my own intellect, to thinking by the eternal principles of God. I choose to *"let this mind be in me which was in Christ Jesus"* (Philippians 2:5).

I am sure that God wants all of us to enter into this realm of believing. Yes, we were saved because we believed, but that doesn't necessarily make us a Believer in the impossible. Yet it's God's pure delight for everyone to become Believers in the impossible. You see believing is where God lives. It *is* His world. He wants to show us how He lives and what His ways are like, and how all things are possible when we believe. God has been waiting for some time to show us how to grow in this realm of the eternal principles of believing because this is His image in the earth and the earth is groaning for the manifestations of the sons and daughters of God. And it takes believing the impossible to demonstrate what you were called to do.

I often hear people say that they are blessed, and I truly believe them because they have God in their lives, but are they Believers? Do they make things happen? Because of their belief, is God moving on their behalf? In reality, when a person is a Believer, they will cause things to happen, whereas those that aren't a Believer are just sitting and waiting for God to do it for them. When we truly believe something, we act on it. We step out to do it. We believe it so much that we cannot just sit as though we don't believe. It's true that sometimes it is something that God has to do but often we haven't done our part to believe and make a way for Him to funnel it to us. Honestly, if we wait until we can see it before we believe it then we are not Believers. A true Believer will stand on what they believe until it manifests.

Truly you are blessed if you believe!

INTRODUCTION

Let's face it, we all struggle with the Adamic nature. We didn't ask for it, but we were born into it. In this book I am candid about my walk with God. There are many of my journal entries that reveal my own struggles with doubt and unbelief. Some entries contain God given revelations that enabled me to overcome and walk by faith. Many times, because of these revelations, I have stepped over into the kingdom realm of believing, and that is the spiritual side of me. Yet on the other side, I have had to wrestle with my thoughts and learn how to govern the wrong thoughts that kept me bound to the fleshly nature of unbelief.

We say that we want to be like Jesus, so if we do, we must learn how to believe in who our Father is. That was the very core of Jesus' message on earth—to believe in Abba Father. On numerous occasions Jesus even stated that it was His assignment in the earth. Everything He did was to glorify God, to do the will of His Father, and to make the people to believe in Abba and who they are in Him. Once Jesus' disciples knew who He was and fully believed, Jesus was crucified within hours. His work was done. Now man not only fully believed on the Lord Jesus Christ as the Son of God, but they also believed that God had sent Jesus because of His love for mankind.

In this book I portray many struggles and battles with doubt and unbelief, but I also give the revelations that have enabled me to conquer. I refuse to give in to unbelief. If I fail at it, then I get up and pursue even harder to be a Believer. I know that it is the only way that I can experience God in the way that I desire. I know that I am created by God to walk in the supernatural so I say to myself, "I can do this! The Word of God does not lie, and it tells *me* that all things are possible if I only believe."

I am sure that you struggle with thoughts of unbelief, yet you are called to be a Believer. You will learn to walk free when you break the cycles unbelief by choosing to become a Believer. I encourage you to let this mind (God's thoughts) be in you which was in Christ Jesus. It is your faith, your trust, your believing, and your thought patterns that become intertwined as you conquer unbelief. You were created by God to walk in the supernatural things of God. Therefore, I am declaring that as you read this book God will give you the keys of believing in the impossible. And I fully believe that you will do it!

I want you to know that I believe in you. I believe that you will become the Believer God intended you to be. And when you conquer unbelief then nothing shall be impossible to you. You are truly blessed because you believe!

Privilege of Believing

We are so blessed to be made in the image of God. The angels do not have this awesome privilege.

We are so blessed that God sent His only Son to redeem us from our sins and to give us life eternal. The demons do not have this privilege.

We are so blessed that we are given the ability to believe and watch it happen. The animals do not have this privilege.

We are so blessed to have the mind that was in Christ Jesus that enables us to know the thoughts of God. From that, we can create our own world.

I could go on and on at how blessed we are and yet we are still living so far beneath the privileges that God has already provided to us.

The Bible is clear at what simple believing can do. It was Jesus Himself that said that *all* things are possible to those who believe (Mark 9:23). So, if we want to get to the place of the endless possibilities, then we must examine what we think, what we trust, and what we believe. Jesus believed and He did great exploits for our Father. He spent His time on earth for the purposes of doing the works of His Father to prove that He was sent by His Father to us, thereby causing people to believe in Him (John 5:36). This *was* His works (John 10:25, 37-38). This is why the priesthood, scribes, and Pharisees sought to kill Jesus because He was teaching the people how to believe and how to walk out what they believed

(John 10:39-42). Jesus was indeed making Believers.

In the 9th chapter of John, Jesus heals a blind man on the Sabbath day, and afterwards, this man was brought before the Pharisees to explain how he could see when he was born blind from his mother's womb. This man could only answer that all he knew was that he was once blind, but now he sees. This angered the Pharisees and they brought forth his parents to confirm that he was born blind. The real issue here was that they wanted to know how he received his sight. What was it that caused his eyes to see? And who did this? After the interrogation the man was set free and Jesus came to the man and from that moment on the once blind man believed on the Lord Jesus Christ and caused others to believe.

In John 11:47-48 the story is told of Jesus resurrecting Lazarus and then a great upheaval came from the chief priests and Pharisees insomuch that they formed a council. Many in this council stated that if they didn't do something that *all* people everywhere would become Believers. Because of this, they sought to kill Jesus. They even sought to kill Lazarus after he was raised from the dead because the resurrection caused many people to believe on the Lord Jesus Christ (John 12:10-11).

Many times, Jesus had to slip through the crowds to avoid death, persecution, or questioning, but this never stopped Him from doing the works of His Father (John 8:59). He was about His Father's business to cause all people to believe that God was their Living God and that He was there for them. Just because the works Jesus did had never been done before, and was in the realm of the impossibilities, the leaders of the day wanted to discredit this nonsense of believing in a God that could do anything—and did! Furthermore, it enraged the chief priests, Pharisees, and Sadducees because Jesus confessed to be the Son of God. They said it was blasphemous (Matthew 9:2-8; 27:43), yet they couldn't deny the power, the wisdom, and the teachings that exuded from Jesus.

Now in our day, we are defined that we are a Believer when we are saved and confessing Jesus is our personal Lord and Savior—and this indeed is a very true statement. The second definition of a Believer comes when we are taught about the gifts. We are often told to believe for healings or miracles—and again, this is a true statement and it's good. However, I'm here to tell you that there is so much more to this equation of becoming a Believer. As Christians, most of us do not believe for signs, wonders, miracles, healings, or the greater works because we simply don't know how. Yet we are born to walk in this privilege of being a Believer. So, I'm telling you, "You can do it! You were, and are, destined to be a Believer."

BECOMING A BELIEVER

Ask yourself this question, "What if I truly believed that when I prayed to God that something would really happen? Do I think that it's even possible?" But don't just leave it there. Go on and ask yourself, "What is the harm in my believing? If I believed and nothing happened then at least I had a chance, but if I don't believe then could there even be a chance? What could it hurt if I choose to believe?"

Let's face it, we all have struggled with unbelief. And even if we conquer unbelief in one area, there are many other areas to conquer. God has been speaking to me about believing and trusting Him for a long time, and assuredly He has been speaking to you about the same things. Here is a journal entry that I entitled, "God calling us to be Believers."

> God keeps speaking to me "Believe." I know that God moves when we believe yet many Christians operate carnally. We do not believe we can do what God says. But if we can believe, then we can do all things because what a man thinks in his heart, so is he (Proverbs 23:7). If a person believes in his heart and confesses with his mouth that Jesus Christ is Lord, then he is saved (Romans 10:8-10). Our works then *is* our believing. Our believing proves our faith and causes it to manifest.

The supernatural order is that hope comes before faith and faith before believing (Hebrews 11:1). Sadly, so many of us have lost our hope that faith is nowhere on the scope and becoming a Believer is forgotten. But I see that God is about to circumvent the supernatural order to jump start the people into believing so that faith and hope will follow and His plan on earth can be accomplished.

God knows that we struggle but He waits for us to put Him to the test. He can and does move by our believing. God wants us to walk in what we know to do and believe Him for the miracles. Some years ago, I had this revelation:

What if God waited for a manifestation before He would believe or act on something? Then something would be terribly wrong! If God had never spoken, nothing would be here. He had to speak it out for any and all things to manifest.

As sons and daughters, we're not supposed to wait to see something before we act on God's Word. God is our Father and He led the way for us. He first demonstrated by speaking the Word, and then watched it manifest. Then He wrote down His Word for us so we could act like Him! We must learn how to cast down unbelief if we are going to walk as sons and daughters and demonstrate the kingdom of God on earth.

I don't know about you but I'm ecstatic to be a child of God! I get the privileges of being His daughter. He has given me the right to believe and see it manifest—but the good news is that He has given that privilege to all of us. Truthfully, all of us have problems that need a solution. We can face those problems with confidence when we believe despite what our eyes see, what our ears hear, and what our intellect is telling us.

I too have missed the mark of believing what God has said (as though He could or would lie) so God gently spoke to me as a Father to their child, "My precious child I love you. You often speak my Words, but I want you to believe them. I am doing for you the unseen. Ask me for a supernatural vision, ask me for a supernatural voice." I had no idea that though I was speaking God's Word, I didn't truly believe in what I was speaking—but God knew it. As a loving Father, He was pointing out that I often quoted His Word and would try so hard to make it work. Mentally I thought, well if I can speak the Word of God enough then it will happen, but in my heart, I knew that I was struggling to believe. As a result, many of my prayers went unanswered because I didn't really believe. The prayers that were answered were because God is sovereign and chose to do so despite my inability to believe.

Like many others I questioned if God would really answer my prayers. God heard me and began to question me, "Why won't you believe that I will do it for you? Didn't you ask me? I need you to believe in your own prayers." I was so humbled and shocked by God questioning me that I quickly repented in my heart, but my mouth couldn't utter a word. Sure enough it wasn't long before I saw the beauty of how God had changed the situation I was petitioning and questioning Him over.

Much time went by after this, and once again because I am human, I lost belief—especially in myself. So, God spoke to me again and said, "You must believe in yourself. I believe in you, you can do anything, yet you still struggle."

Now this really built my belief in myself to know that God believed in me. In *me*! How awesome that we can overlook the fact that God believes in us more than we believe in ourselves, or even in our own prayers?! Yet as time passed, I once again was struggling to believe, so I went to God in prayer. Following is another entry of how God loves us so much and how much He wants us to get to the place of unwavering faith:

In prayer I was crying from being overwhelmed with many things I needed to do but couldn't seem to make them happen. The Lord reminded me that His plan is always bigger than mine; and because it's bigger than me—and because it is His plan, it *will* work. But He also reminded me that "*only* His plan will work" and He is the one responsible. Then I repented before Him.

Jesus began speaking, "*I* am leading you. *I* will give you directions. Everything is in *my* time and in *my* way. Lose your fears, lose your concerns. It will come together as *I* choose. Your part is to believe and walk out what you know. Do not question what you shall say. You will know it when the time comes.

I am still developing you. Right now you are seeing my big plans unfold before you. They look insurmountable, but that's because it is my plan. It's just one day at a time, one step at a time. Confess your victory over what I am giving to you. As you confess it, believe that it will manifest. Do not worry about these things but hear my voice to come closer. I desire you, I desire your worship."

Wow! What an awesome privilege that God believes in us, trusts in us, has patience with us, even when we don't believe. Despite how many times we fail He proves Himself to us again and reminds us how important we are to Him.

God wants us to believe in our own prayers and to believe that we can overcome any obstacles. How great is it that He desires us to get it more than we do! We are truly blessed if we believe that God will do it for us.

No Slave to Doubt and Unbelief

Unlike Jesus, we were all born with the Adamic nature, so we were inherently a slave to doubt and unbelief from our conception. Therefore, we are often unable to recognize how many ways in which doubt and unbelief creeps in, and in how it keeps us from receiving God's ways. God can be trying to give us more faith or help us to believe but we cannot recognize that is what's happening. As a result, we often miss our blessings.

The believing blessing is generally masked by our problems and circumstances that need God's intervention. The reality is that many times we have had to struggle so long in waiting to see the answer come that we get used to seeing the problems and we drown in them, forgetting about the blessings that are to come. We totally lose sight, or lose our belief, that a blessing could possibly come through what we are seeing and experiencing. I too had lost sight of my blessings to come because I had seen the problems for so long that I was failing to believe anymore, but God was gracious to give me this revelation:

> Today the Lord said, "All blessings come from me. I am ready to pour out my blessings upon you. Will you

receive?" I said, "Yes Lord." Then He said, "Do you trust me to bless you?" I said, "Yes, Lord." He said, "To trust me is to have faith in me. Do you believe that now is the time to receive?" I said, "Yes Lord."

This is the revelation that came forth. To have faith is futuristic. Doubt is like chains, it focuses you on the past or present, and is always negative. Believing is always now, and always positive. Doubt has no power other than what we give it. We are in a tug of war with faith versus doubt. Doubt cannot win unless we give it power. Faith has power of its own and when we team up with it, doubt always loses. Faith is what we strive for. I see faith as the prize before us. Doubt as the sin behind us. Believing as the power within us. The Lord keeps on speaking, "Do you trust me? Trust is faith. Believing is the transportation."

After this, I really had to weigh my thoughts in what I believed. I did not want the chains of doubt and unbelief nor the negativity that it hosts. I was more determined than ever to not let doubt have any power that belonged to me. I was ready for faith and belief to win the war. Though the struggles remained, I chose to continue fighting the good fight of faith until I saw the victory.

As the years passed by and other situations came, I eventually forgot that I had promised to trust Jesus. Once again doubt followed me like a mad dog, so one day in my prayer time Jesus said:

"Come into my presence where there is fullness of joy. Here is where you will find the peace you desire. Leave behind the opinions and thoughts of others and know that I am with you. Have I not promised to be with you? Have I not promised that I would not let you make a mistake? Regardless of what others speak, trust in me, trust in my

Word. You have been worried about many things—don't be. Trust only in what I tell you. Yes, I may speak through others to you, but you will know my voice. Trust me that I am able to deliver you from the snare?" (Yes, I do.) "Then your word of agreement is all I need for the door to be open to do so. Trust me that I am able to deliver?" (Yes Lord.) "Then that is all I need to proceed because you have given me an open door. Others may not understand how you can be calm in a storm, but when you rest in me, you will sense no danger. Some people come to change your focus, others your vision, but in my rest your ability to discern will be great. Have I not said, 'Fret not because of evil doers?'" (Yes Lord.) "Then why do you fret? Come into me and I will give you rest."

"Release your weights to me. I am doing a work in your family, so allow me to do more with your faith. Lift up your shield of faith and I will attack your enemies. Do you believe me?" (Yes Lord.) "Now release to me the little foxes that are spoiling my vine (which is you). You are my precious vine whom I love much. Therefore, I purge you much to bring forth fruit for my own pleasure. Undue cares, concerns, and worries release to me. Make faith confessions a part of your everyday language for I desire to invade your life with blessings untold. I have given you no task that I myself will not be involved in."

The fact that Jesus had that much compassion, care, and concern, as well as much patience with me is mind boggling. It's amazing how we can hear the Word of God and go away and forget what He said the first time. So He comes again and very gently reminds us of these important things because He doesn't want us to be enslaved to doubt.

However, He still requires us to make faith proclamations in seemingly hopeless situations for the blessings to come. Then He reassures us that He wouldn't give us any task, or require anything of us, that He wouldn't personally be involved in—and nothing is mightier than Him! We do get weary because the trials can be long and hard, so it takes strength to keep on going and God knows that. I too have had to walk with proclamations while seeing nothing happening. It can be wearisome.

The struggle with the Adamic nature is real. We often walk the path of faith for a while and then fall off. We are all guilty of not overcoming even the smallest of confrontations and situations. Following is another God-given revelation which helped me to progress into believing more, how to rest in His sovereignty, and how to not get stuck in seemingly hopeless situations.

> It takes a strong faith to believe against all odds. Weak faith wavers like the sea; and like a candle it goes out with the slightest puff of wind (James 1:6). Strong faith is like a beacon shining in the night. Weak faith becomes a strong faith when we choose to believe against all odds; when everyone is saying to give up and walk away.
>
> The greatest test of faith comes when, despite your believing, it ends with your deepest faith not manifesting the results you believed for. That's when faith must come to rest in the sovereignty of God. You believe you have failed the test of great faith—but on the contrary. You have overcome doubt, discouragement, confusion, distractions, and have kept your focus on Christ, despite the outcome. Faith has had its perfect work. It has taught you to stay focused on Christ until you came to see Him in the throne room of His sovereignty and grace. We must learn to rest in His decisions. The important thing is that our faith was strengthened to withstand the obstacles that we faced. Herein is our overcoming.

As Daniel, we are to keep looking—not to be fixated on what we are seeing but believing that what we are believing for will manifest. When we keep looking, this is focusing on Christ. If we are to rule and reign with Christ in His throne, we must learn how to overcome (Revelation 3:21). Those with shallow experiences will quit looking. They will quit trying.

There was a son that believed his mother would be resurrected because of a dream he saw. He believed against all odds. Yet when he prayed, she wasn't resurrected. There was a mother believing for her son's healing until the day he died. She believed for years when no one else believed. Yet her son was never healed. There is a wife that has been believing for years for her husband to be a good father that loves to interact with his children. Are these things wrong to believe for? Absolutely not! It takes little faith to believe for a short while.

So today I began to see that we commit the sin of unbelief more than any other sin. The son was not wrong to believe to the end, neither was the mother wrong to believe until the end. So too must others believe. Some will say, "When is that lady going to come to the reality that her husband is never going to do any better?" Therefore, I say that often what we call reality is contradictory to faith. When will we cause our so-called human reality to die in the arms of faith?

I too have been guilty of unbelief; unbelief that the finances due me is for today, thinking of it as futuristic only. Unbelief that today is the day for reconciliation in my family or total health in my body, and more. I have repented.

As God spoke to me a couple of years ago that the

church was using Him as an idol. They act like He is dead, and He cannot see what they are doing or hear their prayers. To them He is a virtual God. This is unbelief. I choose today to repent and begin to believe God. It is time for us, the church, to walk in His manifested presence and believe in Him for who He is.

I do believe that we should support those that are endeavoring to walk by faith, even though we may not see if what they're believing in is true. It's their faith walk—not ours. It's their trials and test of faith—not ours.

God is sovereign and He may choose to hold the answers to our prayers for building a greater and stronger faith in us, more resting in Him, or more patience with others. Even the Patriarchs of old died not having seen or obtained the promises and blessings they thought they would see in their lifetime. But one thing is clear, that to obtain that unwavering faith requires a test of time to build endurance in us, for us to trust God even when we can't see the answers in sight (James 1:6-8). And it's when your faith is strong that doubt loses its power.

I often tell myself when doubt rears its ugly head, "I see what I see—but I know what I know. I know what God has said and I'm not moving off that confession." Doubt and unbelief diminish as I make this confession and I begin to feel stronger within.

Galatians 3:23 says, *"But before faith came, we were kept under the law, shut up unto the faith which should afterwards be revealed."* Galatians 4:3 says, *"Even so we, when we were children, were in bondage under the elements of the world:"* Galatians 4:7 says, *"Wherefore thou art no more a servant, but a son; and if a son, then an heir of God through Christ."* Here we see that the apostle Paul draws a distinct, defining line between the law and faith. Under the law we were in bondage, so we were confined to doubt and unbelief as a prisoner. But now that Jesus came, we are in a faith dispensation, not just grace. Under the faith dispensation <u>we are free</u>

to believe, free to act as sons and daughters of God by our believing that we can do all things through Christ who strengthens us.

Without faith, without believing, we are held in bondage as a slave—a slave to doubt, fear, and unbelief. But now, by our faith, by our believing, we no longer can be held in bondage unless we choose to not let our thoughts be conformed to Christ's. If or when we choose not to believe, we keep ourselves in bondage. Romans 8:2 says, *"For the law of the Spirit of life in Christ Jesus hath made me free from the law of sin and death,"* but I declare unto you that you are made free from all bondages, all slaveries in Jesus' name!

Transforming Your Thoughts

In becoming a Believer, we must stop to think about what we think about. When we've failed, do we take an inventory or assessment of where we've missed it and what we could have done differently? Have you ever analyzed what your thought process was as to why you made the decisions you made? I'm sure you have. You have no doubt wanted to change the outcome of your decisions, but you couldn't because your decisions had brought you to this point. It's then that you decided you needed to make better choices.

To become a Believer, it is critical to change our thought life. Making the choice is easy but it's difficult to follow through. It requires discipline to govern what we think and how often we think it, which is why we often allow our thoughts to control us, instead of us controlling our thoughts. The enemy of our soul knows this human flaw, so he fully intends to capitalize on it.

Before our thoughts can change, we must be aware that they need changing. This is true about anything in life. Changing our thought life first begins in the brain, in the choice to govern what we think and how often we think it. Continual new thought patterns will change the heart, but we must still contend with the old thoughts we don't want. The Bible says in

Proverbs 23:7 that as a man thinks in his heart, so is he. Therefore, any changes that happen in our lives will begin in our heart. That's why I often pray, "God, tell me what I'm thinking that needs to be changed." Then He lets me know through a dream, song, message, friend, prophecy, circumstances, etc. what He desires to be changed. In reality, God wants to help us more than we want to help ourselves, so He delights in teaching us how to govern our thoughts.

One of my biggest strongholds was to believe in my own prayers. Some years ago there was a difficult situation in my life that was very painful, and I prayed earnestly for God to move on my behalf. Over time things got better but I never knew when I would be faced with another similar situation and I certainly didn't want to go through that heartbreak again. As time passed by and things smoothed out, I didn't think about what happened years earlier and I forgot about the prayers. Although things were good, it was like an undercurrent of anxiousness existed that I didn't realize was there—until one day. Sure enough, God knew what was in my heart and that I didn't really believe that He had answered my prayers for change. Once again, I was faced with a situation like unto the first, but I feared the outcome would be the same as before. That's when I began to intercede for God to move on my behalf.

But guess what?

God spoke to me, "Why can't you believe in your own prayers? Didn't you ask me to do this for you?" I humbly replied, "Yes Lord." "So why won't you believe that I have answered you?" I was so stunned that I was speechless. Then He said, "Believe me that I have answered your prayers."

Again, I didn't know that I wasn't trusting God. I didn't know that I wasn't believing that He had answered me until the test came again and I was faced with what was in my heart. I discovered that unbelief existed in me, that I was living in fear, and that fear had become the undercurrent of my life. After God spoke this, I made the choice to trust Him and I stepped out by faith to act as though everything was normal. However, I cannot say that I was stepping out in full faith, nor can I say that I was stepping out in total belief. Nevertheless, I made the choice to believe God and to overcome my fear and confront the situation. When I did, I was amazed that the results were completely opposite of what I had formerly expected.

That night in prayer, I wept before the Lord. Partly because I was so grateful that He had answered my prayers, partly because I was relieved of the fear and anxiousness that had resided in my heart for years, but mostly because I knew I had fallen way short of believing in Him. So my prayer was with tears of thankfulness and repentance. What I had thought was going to be a bad thing turned to be a blessing. I didn't know that my thoughts on the matter needed to be changed, but God knew. He already knew what I was thinking. It's like David said in Psalm 139:1-2, *"O Lord, You have searched me and known me. You know my sitting down and my rising up; You understand my thought afar off."* For sure, God knew my thoughts and knew they needed changing.

Had God not created another situation like unto the first, I would never have petitioned Him. I would have never known of the undercurrent of doubt and unbelief working in me. God, though, loved me enough to reveal this hidden secret. He so proudly wanted me to see how He had answered my prayers, but more than that, He had purposely created a divine appointment so that I could grow in my belief in Him. He is so awesome! It's important to God that we believe in Him, and it's equally important for us to tell Him, "I believe in You." God will rock the world for the one who will choose to believe in Him no matter what. Though it looked bad to me at the onset, I am so grateful that God created the situation just because He loved me so.

I encourage you to begin obeying the scripture in Philippians 2:5 which says, *"Let this mind be in you, which was also in Christ Jesus."* Let Him transform your thoughts. Allow Him permission to renew your mind. He can and will change the outcome of all your decisions if you will allow Him to teach you how govern your thoughts. Remember, what you think matters. Your believing in God is your greatest tool to overcoming, walking with Him, and defeating the kingdom of darkness. Think on these things.

Believing from the Heart

As formerly stated, to begin the process of believing for the impossibilities, we must first begin in our thought life. We must make up our minds to let our choice be to believe. As we continue to believe in our thought life, the believing will begin to settle into our hearts where real and lasting changes occur. Our heart is always the motivating factor. It is the control tower of our emotions, our passions, and our pursuits. Whatever our heart engages in, our actions will soon follow.

In Matthew 22:31 Jesus said to love the Lord your God with all your heart and with all your soul and with all your mind (paraphrased). The pitfall that Christians can fall into after getting saved is in serving God by their own intellect. Though intellect is necessary in coming to know who God is, we must remember that we were only saved because of our heart, not because of our intellect. Therefore, we are to serve by our heart. Servitude by the heart will take us into the realms of the impossibilities, whereas the intellect will always try to logically reason it out. Following is another revelatory journal entry of how our heart must be engaged in order to become a true Believer and to see the manifestations.

If you hear the Word of God with your head and don't

include your heart, your belief system will be based on intelligence alone. But Biblically speaking, your heart is always the control tower, not your head. It's sort of like you're flying a plane and you use only your instruments and never listen to the control tower. If you do that most any dangerous event can happen. So, relying on your intelligence alone can bring destruction if your heart isn't engaged.

Many times, we think we believe and even say that we believe, yet our actions and our works reflect unbelief. It's common for our confession of belief to say one thing, but when put to the test we say another. We could say that the church will grow and believe it while we're in church services but when obstacles come, we say we can't grow because… But Jesus said, "If you can believe, all things are possible," so in essence do we really believe?

The core of Christianity is based on believing from the heart. If a person does not believe in God, they cannot be saved unless they change what they believe. People who don't believe in the baptism of the Holy Ghost will likely never receive Him. And people who don't believe in healings are not likely to be healed unless someone believes for them or God acts sovereignly. So, our belief system comes from our heart and is what we speak.

If a person tries to calculate God intellectually to get saved, they cannot get there. They must include the heart in the equation. You must hear God with your heart because your spiritual ears are on your heart, not your head. This is how your heart can hear from the heart of God (Romans 10:8-10).

Since God is a God of love and our heart is a symbol of love, when we listen with the heart of love, we will hear the voice of God. When listening with our heart, we will never doubt God. Listening attentively and acting upon what He says will cause any unbelief to vanish because the voice of God silences all other sounds. Don't calculate from your head but listen from your heart so that you may be able to overcome unbelief. In essence, don't try to figure out a miracle by your own intellect what God is capable of doing or is going to do. It's more a matter of the heart.

Again, the core of our Christian walk is based upon believing from our heart. Once we believe, and accept Christ as our Lord, we can come to learn of Him both intellectually and spiritually by the heart. Therefore, in order to activate believing, we must engage our hearts. You may ask, "How can I truly believe from my heart so that I can see the manifestations?" Following is one example at how I understood how to grow my belief.

Some years ago, my husband and I were selling jewelry to finance our ministry. We were taking a trip out of town and I wanted to take some rings to sell. As I prayed, I told God that I wanted to sell ten sets of rings, but God revealed to me that in my heart I truly didn't believe that I would, or could, sell that many. He asked me, "What do you really believe with all your heart?" My answer was, "Only two, Lord. Only two sets of rings." He responded with, "Then bring two sets. Let's start here in growing your faith."

I took the two sets of rings with me and I had no problems selling those and no one else even inquired. I came home with this understanding, that what I really believed in my heart was real faith. I could have brought ten sets and sold none because I would have been operating by hope, a hope that I could sell any of them. But when I narrowed it down to what I really, really believed in my heart, that is what activated the manifestation. Then I knew that my believing from my heart is what had activated the transactions.

I truly believe that if we can grab ahold of believing from our heart, that we will see many things manifesting and our faith will grow exponentially. But if you are having a difficult time believing what you should be believing for, it is not shameful to ask the Lord, "Lord, help my unbelief!" I can assure you that God will be delighted in helping you. God is looking for what is happening in your heart and He is wanting to grow your believing in Him for the miracles!

How Believing Multiplies

Once you begin to believe, even for the smallest of things, you will find that it opens the doorway to believe more. Yes, there will always be struggles to believe as you conquer each new territory but once you conquer it your believing will get easier. Eventually you will notice that you are moving effortlessly in that specific area.

This next revelation came as a result in me failing miserably at believing in someone I loved, and I had started accusing them of what they were innocent of. I knew the spirit of accusation was at work and that I had fallen prey to Satan's devices. I was so ashamed and broken and I felt there was no way that I could repair the damage that I had done so God graciously gave me this dream and I journaled:

> Yesterday I had a bad situation that I complicated, and I wept bitterly over it so last night God gave me a dream to comfort me. In this dream God showed me one bad situation after another that was compounded (multiplied) by my inability to handle properly. After each bad situation I would weep, humble myself before Him, and repent. Each time I did this God would work on my behalf and

correct every situation—and He even showed it to me as a math problem.

It was like the situation was -2,000 plus my response of -20,000 to equal -22,000. But when I would repent God would add to my situation according to His math (which is always a positive to the highest degree). This is what it was like: 1,000,000,000,000,000 but on and on because God was in it. I could never have enough negatives to override the pluses of God. All night long God was revealing to me that He is the "Master Mathematician." Yet I knew that as long as I repented God would correct all the damages that I had done.

What I had seen as a multiplication in the most negative degree, I could now believe that God could correct it. To Him it was just a math problem. I had failed to believe that God could do anything with my situation, but God was assuring me that He could make it as though it had never happened, and even better. As I have meditated on this for many years, I realized that our Master Mathematician can do anything. I choose to believe in the impossible even in the most negative situations, and even those that I have brought upon myself.

As the years have passed, that one dream has stayed with me and has helped me to believe against all odds. Unlike us, I don't think that Jesus ever had a struggle believing in any area. Jesus simply believed. Furthermore, His miracles caused believing to increase among His followers until they became Believers in the impossibilities. Those miracles He performed were most often multiplied. The following journal entry contains information I discovered on the website concerning God's math and His multiplication abilities. This helped me even more to understand our Great Master Mathematician.

God is taking me back to school; only this time, it's His

way. I have been praying much about having the thoughts of God; having the mind of Christ. So last night I was doing research when I came across a website called *Transforming Teachers*. The writer begins to explain that God's principles are foundational in everything. On the subject of math, the writer explains how math alone proves the existence of God and His attributes. It proves all the science of creation by math.

He described how man has taken the credit for math, and that if man ceased to exist, so would math since man created it. I had no idea that man took credit for something that is so simple and complicated at the same time. Numbers never end—which is a true picture of God.

In this article, the author describes how to retrain the mindset of the teachers. That the Bible is the final authority, and thus, the principles therein are the teacher in itself. The author goes on to say that man has taken the approach that we take the world's system of math, the world's foundation of math, and make the Biblical principles apply and call it Christian Education. The writer goes on saying that since God is the Creator of all things—and sets our principles for us, that His math is the only true math. It further describes that we are to look at His math and its principles and use God's system, apply His principles, and they will work far better.

My first thought was how Jesus turned the water into wine. It was a single—yet multiple miracles simultaneously. It was deemed as one miracle, yet there was no way to count how many bottles were turned to wine. The same goes for the widow woman and the cruise of oil. A single miracle is deemed, yet how many times did she pour out oil? How many more cakes did she make? I thought about Gideon.

Less is more. God didn't need thirty thousand, He only needed three hundred, and actually He could have done it with three if He had wanted to—or none at all! But the most profound thought was Jesus feeding the five thousand or the three thousand with simply a piece of fish and a loaf of bread—and then had twelve baskets of leftovers!

Look at Jesus with the woman at the well, the Samaritan woman. When the disciples came back from town with food, Jesus had no need of it and the disciples were baffled because they knew that Jesus had not eaten. Jesus' reply was, *"I have food to eat that you know not of"* (John 4:32, paraphrased). Jesus had a way of eating and sustaining life purely by knowing how to digest the Word of God. At one point Jesus said, *"...Man shall not live by bread alone, but by every word that proceeds from the mouth of God"* (Matthew 4:4). Somehow Jesus had spiritual food that sustained His natural body.

When Jesus spoke about feeding the five thousand, He had not eaten in three days either and had been pouring out of His spirit. This would exhaust us. But Jesus' ability was based on the knowledge of the thoughts of God. He could sustain the body for much longer period than man because He knew God's math. It did not take natural food to sustain life. He was the second Adam. He walked with God as did Adam and Eve in the garden. Yet Jesus spoke the principles of God (which contains the math element) and reproduced the amount of food required to feed five thousand people and still gathered twelve baskets of food to complete the miracle.

So last night I realized that I need to understand God's math all the more. I need to be retrained. Only then can I see the multiplicity of God's numbers manifest. The understanding of His math will silence that voice of the negative numbers of bad situations concerning people, money, or any situations. Now I'm in a good school—God's school!

I am convinced that as we learn to exercise our believing, we should expect it to multiply, not multiplying according to the math of this world, but according to the math of God's eternal principles, which is always abundant. He is always more than enough. This is what Jesus did.

I challenge you to test the believing principles of the eternal math by speaking positive over your negative situations. Expect the Master Mathematician to multiply your believing, multiply your miracles, and multiply your abilities in the impossibilities. Expect Him to bring His positive multiplications into your situations in your favor until you have leftovers. Truly you are blessed if you can believe!

Jesus' Works of Believing

So often we don't see what is in plain sight. Many times, John the beloved recorded the mission of Jesus to cause all people to believe. We can say that Jesus' mission was to redeem the loss—and yes it was. But in order to accomplish what He came to do, He had to first make people believe in who He was and why He came. He could have done it all, but unless He taught us to believe, we would not have received any benefits of what He did. It is on the premise of believing that heaven becomes our home and the kingdom manifests on earth. Jesus had to make Believers by what He did so we all could inherit eternal life. Therefore, Jesus went about performing miracles to prove who He was so that we could become a Believer.

Over and over Jesus made it abundantly clear that He only said what He heard His Father saying or did what He saw His Father doing. He clearly communicated to the people that the Father sent Him because He loved us. Therefore, all the works that Jesus performed was to cause people to believe in Him. Once they became Believers Jesus taught that they too could perform the works of the Father. Jesus would impart to them, and then send out those Believers to declare the kingdom of heaven has come, then they healed the sick, raised the dead, and did cast out many demons. God's ultimate plan was to evangelize the world with the Good News (the Gospel) until everyone was reached. The mission was to make the whole world Believers in God and who they were in Him. It is for this purpose that the gospels record many instances of Jesus' miracles and healings.

Let's look at another side to Jesus' works. In the midst of performing the healings and miracles, many leaders despised that Jesus was making Believers in God the Father. They confronted Him on many occasions, they openly rebuked Him, and even tried to kill Him because He was making Believers. This is something that we must be prepared to encounter. In reality, some people will readily believe while others may never choose to do so. They may even hate you because of your abilities and your passion to heal the sick, raise the dead, or cast out demons. But never did Jesus allow the negativity to dissuade Him from His purpose, so we must not be discouraged either when we are faced with the same things as Jesus was. Let's look at some prime examples from the book of John.

In John 5:5-10 Jesus asks the impotent man by the pool of Bethesda if he wanted to be made whole. Basically, Jesus was asking if the man believed that He could do it. The Bible says that the man believed on Jesus and was made whole, but afterwards the Pharisees rebuked Jesus for healing on the Sabbath day. The hardness of the Pharisees hearts revealed that unbelief was at the core. Unbelief in the heart is as a tomb within because without belief we are as dead men. Because their hearts were hard and rooted in unbelief, they wanted all people to remain unbelievers as themselves. Unbelievers do not want liberty, nor do they want others to walk as a free person. But believing is the way, the pathway, the road to freedom, deliverance, and joy beyond measure. Believing is the antidote for many anxieties. This lets us know that many are waiting on us to cause them to become a Believer, to deliver them from the unbelievers.

John 4:39 tells us that an entire city believed on Jesus because of the Samaritan woman's testimony of Jesus. This lets us know that we could make just one passionate Believer and it can have a rippling effect. That one Believer can change an entire city or group of people. God plans to use anyone that will choose the mission of making Believers of the Lord Jesus Christ. Not just for the sake of salvation alone, but like the Samaritan woman, for them to quickly take the forefront in the harvest fields for God.

John 4:41-42 says that many people believed what Jesus said. In John 4:49-53, when Jesus declared healing for the nobleman's child, the nobleman believed what Jesus said and his entire household were converted because of his son's healing. Here we see that God is behind the scenes bringing belief in the sinner so that when they hear the Word, they will believe. Sinners typically need to hear the Word, but most need to see manifestations before believing. Jesus knew this which is why He did so many signs, wonders, healings, and miracles because they needed it in order to believe (John 4:48). We must step out on faith to pray for the sick regardless of what others think. It's Jesus' job to do the healing; our job is to pray and believe. The more we do it, the more our faith will grow.

Before Jesus resurrected Lazarus, He publicly prayed so that the people would believe. As soon as Lazarus' was resurrected the Bible says that many Jews believed on Jesus. This alarmed the Pharisees and chief priests and they said, *"If we let him thus alone, all men will believe on him."* When God does the impossibilities, everyone has to take notice. Some will praise God while others may be enraged, as were the chief priests. Now that Lazarus was resurrected and so many people believed, they wanted to kill him so they could take away the belief of those just being converted. Yet the more people see the manifestations of what our Father is saying, the more they will believe and be converted (John 11:42-45, 48).

Although Jesus performed many miracles, still yet there were some who never believed that He was sent by the Father (John 12:37-40). This was a fulfillment of scripture by Isaiah that their eyes would be blinded, and their hearts hardened. This is further evidence that hard hearts cannot believe. Nevertheless, some of the chief rulers did believe on Jesus, but sadly they would not confess Him as their Lord and Savior because they would be put out of the synagogue (John 12:42). They feared being banned from the house of God. Our lesson is, don't worry about the naysayers, they will always be around. Confess you are a Believer and let others do what they do.

In general, people will believe the works before they will believe in Jesus, both sinner and Christian. Even the disciples walking with Jesus, seeing many works, didn't believe on Jesus as the Son of God for three years though He had empowered them to heal the sick, cast out devils, rebuke diseases, and do all the works through His name. This lets us know that we all need to see manifestations, but someone has to believe to begin the process.

Many Christians still struggle with believing because we haven't seen the miracles and healings happening. Or perhaps, we haven't stopped to realize that we are already seeing the miracles. Honestly, many times we don't believe that when we pray that God will answer so we don't try. Yet we are told by God that if we could believe, all things are possible. God is longing for us to just believe in Him and believe that we can walk in the impossibilities.

John 7:38-39 says that he that believes on Jesus, out of his belly shall flow the rivers of living water. This lets us know that if we are saved then we already have the rivers of living waters, we just need to believe. Believing is the waterways. We came into salvation because we believed, so to perform the works of God for the harvest of the kingdom, we have to continue to believe that God is with us. When we enter into a continual state of believing, it gets God's attention and it puts our words into action. It's like words that have been in type written form where the lettering is detached becomes in cursive. When letters are in cursive, they are connecting to one another in unity and the letters flow instead of being disjointed. It's like the words come alive and flows out of you. The rivers of living water that ushers in the healings and miracles are already within us. Our continual state of believing is what makes it flow.

In John 10:25-38 Jesus told the Jews that He was the way to Father God, but they didn't believe Him. Jesus' answer was that even if they couldn't believe that He was the way, that at the very least they could stretch themselves to believe that the works which He did was the works of God and to believe that God was in Him. After seeing the works, they couldn't deny what He said, so many Jews believed on Jesus that very day.

Jesus even questioned His own disciples, *"Do you now believe?"* (John 16:31). The disciples already believed in the works, but Jesus wanted to know if they truly, truly believed that He was sent from God. We too can believe that Jesus came from God, yet because we don't see His works as they did, we fail to believe that we can do what Jesus did. We feel that doing those works are reserved for those ordained and hold the office of the clergy. But Jesus desired that His own disciples would teach others how to believe that they too could do the works of the Father.

In reality, Jesus still imparts to us the same power and authority as He did His disciples, to go into all the world and preach the gospel, for us to fulfill the great commission of reconciling men back to God (2 Corinthians 5:18-19). In order to accomplish this, we too must say what we hear our Father saying, do what we see our Father doing, and go where our Father is sending us. This is the works of God: to do all His good pleasure/will in order for the kingdom to manifest on earth.

After Jesus' death and resurrection, He taught the disciples for 40 days pertaining to the kingdom of God (Acts 1:3). What Jesus' taught is not recorded, but what we do know is that the disciples turned the world upside down and made many Believers, yet they were not the only ones performing miracles.

Jesus said that greater works will we do, but we cannot not do the greater works until we can learn how to do the works. As Jesus, we must know what Daddy God desires us to do. As Jesus, we need a relationship with God to learn of the Father's heart. The works are born from our continual relationship with the Father. Only then will we see a true harvest. We have so often followed others because we have not been taught that we also possess the power for these signs to follow us. God would have all of us to follow after Him and seek Him with our whole heart, then these signs and wonders, healing and miracles would follow us.

Jesus told us of His works and why He did what He did. As we follow His example, we too will do works like Him. We will believe and cause others to believe. I am convinced that God wants us to get it more than we want it. He does not want us to be spiritually deaf or blind but desires us to see and step into what He is doing. He wants us to follow His leading. If we will choose to believe as Jesus did, we can do the same works. As we continue to grow in faith and allow the rivers of living water to flow through us, then great faith will pour from us and we will see the greater works.

Crossing Over to Believing

Crossing over into believing is like crossing over a bridge. On the earthly side, the land you see has been so ravaged by sin that it looks like a war zone and nothing exists but debris. Yet the land is only part of the devastation. The natural body and mindset have been affected and infected with the sin of doubt and unbelief. You feel helpless, hopeless, fearful, and exasperated because nothing is in order. You cannot see where you are or where you're going. You feel that there is no point to life and that life will never get any better.

As you cross the bridge to the other side you will notice that this land is totally different. You have entered into the eternal kingdom of God where the ravages of sin cannot touch. The land itself is at peace and filled with joy; everything is healthy and whole. Here in this place your eternal mindset begins to be renewed with hope, belief, and faith. You can clearly see how things will get better. You begin to get stronger and more hopeful in your mind and spirit, and you feel that you can do anything.

What I have discovered is that we will cross this bridge many times. With each new situation that we face we must once again cross over into believing that God can and will do the impossible. I have also found that we often stand on the bridge not knowing whether to believe or not to believe.

Here is one example that I journaled some years ago and the revelation that poured forth:

> *Crossing Over to Believing (Other People's Physical Healing)*
>
> I was praying for my friend, Sandra, to be healed of cancer and asked God if He wanted to receive her unto Himself or heal her. I didn't know what to believe. I didn't know what to pray. And I didn't know whether to stand in faith to see her miracle. So as I prayed several times about this God gave me the answer I have looked for, for years. This is the answer:
>
> My job is to believe the impossible and to pray for the healing—always! God says in His Word to *"believe that you shall have and you shall receive"* (Mark 11:24) and Hebrews 11:6 says, *"Without faith it is impossible to please God."*
>
> Often the word *will* in the Bible means, *pleasure* or *pleased*. Then whosoever does the will of the Father is doing the pleasures of the Father (Matthew 7:21). I cannot walk in unbelief that God will heal people and be pleasing to God because without faith God is not pleased.
>
> So my job is to believe that it's God's pleasure to heal unless God tells me that it is a sickness unto death. And to walk in faith is to believe the impossible, which is the very thing that pleases Him; to believe that His will is His desire to do it.

This revelation changed my outlook on everything; to learn that my job is just simply to believe that it is God's pleasure to heal. Yet I cannot say that I remained in the land of believing. In reality, it is much easier for us to believe for others to be healed, but when we feel our own pains, we find that we are still living in the land of unbelief. Here I was in full faith that God was going to heal my friend, but I was also in need of healing from a torn rotator cuff in my shoulder and was struggling to believe because of the pain I was experiencing. Once again, I began trying to cross over into the land of believing. Here is another entry that happened just 2 weeks after that mighty revelation that changed my outlook.

Crossing Over to Being a Believer (Personal Physical Healing)

I have been in need of healing from shoulder pain when I came to the point of, "Either I believe, or I don't believe. If I don't believe, then why call myself a Christian because I'm not being Christ-like?" Christ believed that when He prayed that it would happen, so should I.

So, I made up my mind that I would be a Believer. I told God, "I choose to be a Believer. I choose to believe when it looks foolish." The truth is that we either believe or not. Then I made the confession, "I *am* a Believer! I confess—I *am* a Believer!"

The more I confessed "I am a Believer" the stronger I felt in my inner man, and each time I confessed it I could feel God pouring more believing into me. It was like I had opened a door for believing to come inside of me and take up residency. I then decided to keep on confessing so I could stay in the land of believing—and I did for a while. Then it's like I forgot who I was and what I was capable of. (As you well know when you confess that you want to be a Believer, the test is sure to follow.)

I cannot say that I won the battle of believing since I ended with having shoulder surgery. Having surgery then caused another battle—the battle of self-condemnation for not believing enough to avoid the surgery. None the less, I finally resolved that my believing carried me as far as it could, and I commanded myself to just be at peace and to allow my believing to grow. I then came to understand that God uses our willingness to become a Believer to reveal where we aren't believing. He wants us to be a Believer in every area of our life, so He will quickly show us where we need help. He will reveal the problem area only to show us what to do next to be an overcomer and a Believer.

After many times of crossing over and then going backwards to unbelief, I have come to understand that surrendering and humbling myself before God is one of my greatest assets to becoming a Believer. It's true that we can have just one bad experience that cripples us and we don't know how to get back to believing. Yes, we may forgive the person(s) and go on to receive emotional healing. And yes, we may have resolved to letting God take care of that person(s) or situation. Yet to continue to do what you did before, or return to it if you have walked away, you cannot seem to make yourself do it. I too have had situations that crippled me causing me to stop or change directions and as a result, anxiousness came in. Then one day God gave me this revelation:

Surrendering my Control to God (Behavioral Healing)

I had not realized until lately how much I was operating in anxiousness. As God revealed the area, I surrendered and confessed it to God, then I made the choice to release it. Basically, what I saw was that I had one bad experience that kept dragging down my faith to believe that everything will turn out okay (like I am the only one responsible for it all).

A day came that I dared to step back into that specific area, and for the first time in my life, I experienced a true bowing to God. I've always bowed my body to Him with all my heart, in honor and reverence, but this time was so different. It was a humility that I had not experienced before. In my surrender and brokenness, I bowed and felt the presence of God and it was as though I heard Him speak that this is true bowing and worshiping. This surrender was the sweetest and most restful place I've ever known.

It's amazing at how crippling the fear of rejection, hurt, anguish, and other negative emotions can have in our psyche. Even though I knew all of these revelations, and intellectually knew the Word of God, yet it is totally different to believe that everything is going to turn out well, that you can actually expect to succeed where you have once failed or been rejected. So in my prayer time I began beseeching God as to how to overcome the fears. Here is part of a journal entry and what Jesus said about it:

> In 1999 I did a goal setting of what I wanted to accomplish in my life. I didn't just list what I wanted, but also the hindrances and fears that would keep me from accomplishing those goals. It's interesting to note that many times I listed the fear of rejection. At that time, I saw what my fear was and prayed about it, then as the years passed by, I ceased praying and totally forgot about the goal setting. One day I was going through an old spiral bound notebook looking for an entry and came across the goal setting. I was excited when I could clearly see that part of those goals had come to pass without my striving to accomplish any of them. But one thing was powerfully evident, and that was the fear of rejection present in all my goal settings that I had not yet overcome. I seriously began praying and the Lord said this to me, "You must not fear rejection. The world has rejected me and it will certainly reject you. If you fear rejection, then when it comes your worse fear has come upon you and you will be paralyzed. The fear is worse than the rejection itself. You must overcome the fear."

I said all of this to let you know that fear itself gets in the way of us accomplishing what we are put on earth to do. Fear is always present in this earth and will remain until this earth is over. Fear certainly gets in the way of you believing in Jesus, believing in all things good, believing in success, but also in believing in yourself.

After years of seemingly no success in the many areas of ministry that I pursued, I became discouraged and sought God diligently. I prayed to understand how to keep on believing when I could see absolutely nothing happening of what I set my hands to do for Him. Where was it that I was missing Him? Or was it just a test of faith? I, like you, wanted to know what to do next so as I prayed this revelation came:

Believing in Myself (for the promises God made)

Tonight in prayer I asked God if it was wrong to believe in yourself. It seemed anti-Christian since we are to be reliant and believing in God, but He let me know that it is not wrong. In fact, some things of God require that we believe in ourselves before we can see or do what God needs done. This *is* our faith at work.

Abraham had to believe in himself before Sarah could possibly conceive. In Romans 4:17-21 it says that Abraham wrestled with hope to have faith in the now. I came to the point where I asked myself, "So why wouldn't God bless me? And why not believe in myself when God believes in me?" I cast down unbelief and doubt that was imparted to me.

This revelation brought me so much peace because I could totally relate to Abraham. He kept on believing in His promises even though years had passed and he and Sarah were still incapable of conceiving. When all seemed lost, Abraham may have felt unsuccessful, yet he kept on battling unbelief. He stood firm when he could see nothing happening. God had promised a child and now they were both old, but Abraham chose to continue believing in himself that he was capable of having a child and kept on trying. Therefore, I too must begin to confess "I believe" when I cannot see anything happening.

Some years earlier I had a revelation about how our words are more powerful in the spirit realm than we can possibly understand. And in confessing what we believe, how it plays a major role in the heavens which manifests on earth. Here is a revelation that helped me to cast down unbelief:

Our Prayers in the Spirit Realm

In the spirit realm our words are not just sounds. Our words, like God's, have the ability to create. We were made in God's image and in His likeness to do what He does. In Revelation 5:8 it says that our prayers are held in vials. That means that our prayers are tangible in the spirit realm. As we have learned in science classes, matter has substance. So, in the spirit realm our prayers are matter which can be heard, seen, and held in vials. Furthermore, our prayers can be smelled. Revelation 8:3-4 says that our prayers are poured out on the altar of incense and comes up before God as a sweet smell. Therefore, your prayers can be seen, heard, held in vials, poured out, and smelled. When they are poured out upon the altar in heaven, your prayers come up as a memorial for God. We just have to know that God loves our prayers and will honor them in His time and in His way.

You too may have felt like your prayers haven't risen above the ceiling, but know that God holds each and every prayer in a most precious vial with your name on it. I believe that as we confess, "I believe…" that it will strengthen our spirit man and hasten God to our prayers. God knows every weakness that we have and when we fall short of believing. God is still sovereign and can still choose to honor the prayers of a pure heart regardless. It's just that believing gives the open doors for us to receive the answers to those prayers. I believe that our vocal confessions have so much power that we cannot truly comprehend it.

In having the revelation of our prayers in heaven, one day in prayer I began to confess what I believed, and it helped to encourage me as I vocally confessed my belief. As I prayed, I began to tell God all the things that I believed. Some of the things I said were: "I believe that you love me God. I believe that I walk in the miracles and healings now. I believe you are working all things for my good. I believe you hear my prayers and answer me…" On and on I made believing proclamations and it strengthened my spirit man.

What we confess, even if we're not quite there in believing, sets the pathway for that which we believe to manifest. Believing is often progressive and we must make the choice to walk that pathway. It's true that we can hear the Word of God, a message on Sunday morning, and not confess that we believe it, and we often find that we cannot get to where they were trying to take us. That is scriptural. Which is why watching what our mouths speak is so important. Because what we speak is what we will become. Believing is important to receiving the message God is choosing to give us. Believing is important to God and is the pathway for us to receive His promises.

Some years ago, I preached a message and wondered if the people received what was preached. As I shared this with my son he said, "It depends on whether the people will believe the report. If they believe it, they will see it. If not, they won't." I know myself that it is so easy for us to hear a word—and even easier to forget it. Yet to walk as a Believer, the key is to continue working at remembering and believing it.

Many times, I myself have attempted to step over into the realm of believing in what was spoken and have had to fight with the spirit of unbelief. It's important to realize that sometimes you are actually fighting against an ancient spirit of unbelief that came in when Adam and Eve sinned. In reality, all of us have had the doubting Thomas moments and all of us have had to say the prayer of, "Lord, help my unbelief." The battle against the spirit of unbelief is real. Part of our success depends on believing the Word God gave us and acting on it.

As I have stated before that as you begin to cross over into becoming a Believer, the warfare intensifies. The enemy of your soul certainly doesn't want you to know that you have the power over him or the demons. This will be an ongoing battle until the day you die. Many times, I have intensely prayed because I was determined to cross over into the realm of believing despite the battle. Then one day the Lord sent a minister to me to assure me that God was changing the angels that guarded me because of the assignment that He had given. Then Jesus said, "Your job is to do what God asks, and *believe* and walk in love and peace." What a powerful word!

Not long thereafter I began to feel the heavy artillery around me— and the warring angels too. One morning I awoke seeing a vision of angels. In this vision I was on my knees in prayer when the angels began dropping all around me. I could hear, "Thud, thud, thud, thud, thud," as their feet was hitting the ground and the earth shaking. Even in my natural body I could feel the power of God surging through them to me. I felt like I was invincible, like I could literally conquer anything. All I could think of was how God was sending me help, yet my job was only to believe and to do what God asks of me, then walk in love and peace.

What if I had not believed the report of the prophet? What if I had chosen to fight the battles alone by not believing that God would send me help? My job is to do what God has asked of me and believe that all things are possible. When I truly believe, I will be able to walk in love and peace, joy and grace, like never before. Choosing to believe affects everything about how we live, who we become, being healthy, or even how we age. As I've stated before, the sin of unbelief is committed in us far more than we realize.

There are many things that believing confessions do for us.

Remember that life and death is in the tongue (Proverbs 18:21). We should learn to confess holiness, righteousness, health, happiness, joy, peace and more. One thing I chose to do when I was a teenager was to believe and confess that I would never get old. I had started observing people that were so willing to embrace aging and dying. They were always blaming their shortcomings to getting old, yet I couldn't imagine why they would so readily receive that confession. So, I started saying, "I am *never* growing old. My numbers have to change but I don't have to accept old age. Being old is a mindset, so I don't plan to ever get old." I truly believed that confession and I still do. Even today I am quick to correct people that tell me that I'm getting old. Yet I never really thought about getting old as being part of sin and death until the Lord spoke this to me:

> Jesus said, "I am glad that you aren't ashamed of your age. You are quick to refuse to accept old age and you should. Non-acceptance is refusal to let that sin of death affect your thinking.
>
> Your friend Sandra is well. I have answered your prayers concerning her. As you pray for others, you will see many more healings, and miracles come forth. Keep exercising your gift…Guard against speaking the evil of unbelief. Your family will come into alignment as I have purposed, so don't fret over them. Your believing is sufficient.

Again, I know that believing sets the stage for how our youthfulness can remain. But you will notice that Jesus turned the conversation when He spoke. It's always interesting that Jesus most often talks to you about what He wants to talk about and not necessarily what you want to talk about. So, in my prayer time, Jesus just started telling me all this. And not only did Jesus talk about the sin of death by what I thought and believed, but He pointed out that He had already healed my friend. Then went on to tell me to guard what I confessed. It was so powerful that He would speak about my believing being sufficient for anything I needed to happen!

One thing I recently have come to know about believing is that belief existed before time and will exist after this life is over. Since unbelief is based upon the sin principle, then we know that it will not and cannot enter into the kingdom of God but believing will live on in eternity. In fact, we could truthfully say that to believe is life-giving. Have you ever noticed that when you talk doubt and unbelief that you feel deadness and sadness moving inside your body? And have you noticed that when you talk belief in what God can do, you can actually feel life surging inside of you? Some time ago I had this revelation:

Life of God (Believing Brings Life)

Moses was sustained on top of the mountain because he walked *inside* of the Life Giver. Moses did not want to go into the Promised Land if God wasn't going. He would rather die than to not be able to go inside of God. I thought about Jesus being the life and how He proclaimed that He was the Life, and how He sent His life-giving Word to raise Lazarus. I also saw in the fourteenth through sixteenth chapters of John how we are given the promise that if we abide (live) inside of God and God in us that we shall have whatsoever we ask.

As I thought of so many situations in the New Testament of how Jesus gave life, I thought about how my shoulder is experiencing a death that cannot continue in that state because I know the Life-Giver. This is how the disciples began to walk in divine miracles and such. Everything they touched began to *live* again. That's when I realized that becoming a Believer is largely governed by how well we know the One who gives Life.

Knowing the Life-Giver (Jesus) is essential. The more you know God and how He loves you, the more you will learn to believe in what He says is true. God wants to bless us more than we want Him to bless us. In crossing over to be a Believer, it grows as you begin to know God more intimately, believing what He says is true, and then confessing that you believe it.

As I began to share some of these revelations with Bobby, he summed it up this way: The door is the Door of Hope. You cannot go through the door until you grab ahold of faith. Faith is the doorknob. Then it takes trust to step over the threshold; so trust *is* the threshold. After you are on the other side, you are in the place of belief where the glory of God exists.

When you begin to cross over into being a Believer there are many areas to conquer. Whether you think of it as the realm of believing, the land of believing, or the bridge that connects the natural with the supernatural, just know that you are entering into an eternal dimension that cannot be taken away from you. You alone will choose to cross over. You alone will fight the battle of unbelief. You alone can conquer with the help of God.

I encourage you to take the steps to cross that bridge. It will be an internal battle that is affected by external circumstances. I can tell you that staying in the land of doubt and unbelief is tormenting and will discourage you to the point you don't think you can get over the bridge. Take that initiative to confess your own "I believe…" and watch your belief grow. There is fullness of joy for you in God. You just need to make the choice to cross over to a Believer.

KNOWING GOD'S THOUGHTS

God is so great, mighty, and holy, so how can we know His thoughts? How can we attain to His knowledge? In Psalm 92:5 David acknowledges that God's thoughts are very deep, and then in Psalm 139:6 he says, *"Such knowledge is too wonderful for me; it is high, I cannot attain unto it."* The apostle Paul also commented, *"For who hath known the mind of the Lord?..."* (Romans 11:34). All of us can acknowledge that God's thoughts are very deep and high, yet God wants us in His world of thoughts.

Jeremiah cues us into the secret that God wants us to know what He thinks of us and what His plans are for us. Jeremiah heard the voice of the Lord saying to tell His people, *"For I know the thoughts that I think toward you, saith the Lord, thoughts of peace, and not of evil, to give you an expected end."* This lets us know that God wanted His people, and He still does, to know that He does not have thoughts to do us evil, but to give us peace. God plans the very best for us and tells us to expect a good ending to all our problems.

Not only does God want us to know that He's got good plans in store for us, David lets us in on another big secret. God doesn't just think about us every once in a while, He thinks of us *all* the time. Somehow

David understood this and said, *"Many, O LORD my God, are thy wonderful works which thou hast done, and thy thoughts which are to us-ward: they cannot be reckoned up in order unto thee: if I would declare and speak of them, they are more than can be numbered"* (Psalm 40:5). Then on in Psalm 139:17-18 David says, *"How precious also are your thoughts unto me O God! How great is the sum of them! If I should count them, they are more in number than the sand: when I awake, I am still with you."* David had caught a glimpse of our magnificent God and how wonderful His thoughts are towards us and that we couldn't even count the number of times that God thinks about us! If we can believe that God's very deep and very high thoughts are pointed to us-ward, then we are on our way to accomplish great things with Him and through Him. Even now the thoughts that God is thinking towards you is activating you towards His perfect plan.

We must realize that when God thinks about anything, it *will* happen. God's thoughts always precede His works. Being so mighty, God must watch what He thinks because just His thoughts will change everything. Solomon notes this in Proverbs 3:20 when he says, *"By His knowledge the depths are broken up, and the clouds drop down the dew."* How awesome that God's thoughts alone would cause the depths of the sea to break up. Since God's thoughts can do this, then what about His thoughts towards us? What about His plans for us that came out of His thoughts? God knows that for us to walk in the level of belief to do the impossible, then He must allow us to know His thoughts and plans.

Some years ago, in my prayer time God said to me, "Listen to my thoughts for you. Know that I am near, even in your breath and on your lips." I was so blown away with how much God was desiring for me to hear His thoughts concerning me. My mind immediately went to Jeremiah 29:11 at how great His thoughts are for me. Afterwards, I bathed in this Word from God for days and it changed how I thought about myself. I realized that I was thinking less of myself than God was. It amazes me how His love had compelled Him to share His thoughts with me. Again, I'm reminded of how mindful that He is of me.

So what does it feel like to you when He shares His thoughts with you? Often you will feel a warming sensation in your heart or an exhilaration like "Wow! I've never thought of that before." I'd like to share a few of my visions and experiences with you.

> I was in a vision when Jesus spoke, "There is a canopy of love draped around you. There is a fragrance pot in your midst." I saw a huge canopy come down over me like I was in a tent. The color was like a golden yellow. When He spoke of the fragrance pot, I knew He was burning what He liked and I knew it was sweet, yet I did not smell it, I only saw the pot. I felt a warming sensation, yet not from the pot, it was the love and peace that was present. There was no sound. Everything was still, yet it was not a deafening silence. Everything lived, like it was breathing. I knew God was there though I could not see Him. The love was so thick and intense that I needed no one else present to feel loved. I realized that this love has cradled me many times.

Sometimes in a vision, you can understand what you are hearing or seeing, or just a "knowing" in your spirit as to what you are experiencing. In this vision I was both seeing myself from a distance and experiencing walking in under a canopy. I could not smell but I saw and experienced very lively emotions. There was no sound, but no sound was necessary. God had allowed me to experience something wonderful, really wonderful! Then only two days later He allowed me to experience another place that was equally as wonderful. This time, I could see and smell, but again no sounds were necessary.

> Vision in the spirit: I am about to enter a new sanctuary. I smell the perfume. I have never been here before. I see a fruit basket of His presence. I hear, "Oh taste and see

that The Lord is good." The floor is pristine white. A tall floor vase holds all types of fruit. I can smell it. The light just exists, it comes from everywhere. The wind of God lives here. The entire room—walls and all—breathe. The room is open like the ceiling is an open trellis. There are no worries here, just a quiet knowing that all is well, and everything is properly cared for. A quiet joy.

Even though I had these two wonderful experiences, I note that I still live in this world and often forget to allow my spirit to draw from God (which is really all that's necessary; and no words can be spoken to make His presence feel better). So God in His loving ways, spoke this to me while I was in prayer:

"I hunger for your worship. Come higher in me and abandon worries. Have I not told you to 'Fear not?' You know I have. All these things will work out—but don't let them crowd your mind. Many joyous days are here. Don't allow the mysteries of the unsolved to consume you. Speak to them but worship me. Come into my thoughts for you. I feel your sadness but let me have it."

When God spoke this, I didn't catch what He was trying to convey. Sometimes we miss the little details that make the biggest impacts. After a few days I felt compelled to re-read some journal entries and I was wowed. I said, "Wait! What?! God said to come *inside* His thoughts? That's when I caught the revelation and recorded this entry:

I understood that God's thoughts were so big that I could walk inside like it was a large room. Oh, how small my thoughts are! Even I can't fit into my small thoughts! So last night in worship, it's like I went into the room of His thoughts. It was a huge and vast room—and it was so free there. I don't recall seeing anything in there, yet it wasn't empty. The space was filled with just me and Him, so I worshiped Him. There was a light that emanated from everywhere and the room was filled with a serenity beyond anything I've ever known in this world.

I have never thought about God's thoughts like this! That's when years of journaling made another impact. I have recorded how God was always pressing me to think bigger, and after this revelation, I realized that the canopy dream was me *inside* the thoughts of God. Even the sequel dream of a quiet joy was inside the mind of God. All of it began to make sense. Knowing God's thoughts is possible! All of these things began circulating in my mind of how God is so thoughtful of us and has big plans for us, yet we don't experience more because our own thoughts get in the way of God's thoughts or we don't think big enough.

After this experience, I was re-reading my journals when I came across a former dream, and immediately I had the revelation of that dream. (It is important for us to journal even if we don't understand the dream because later God will fit those pieces together like a puzzle). I recorded this:

The Insideness of God

Once I had a dream where Bobby and I were carried to the mountain top, but I didn't understand the dream. Later I understood that it was the mountain of the thoughts of God and that I can only ascend the mountain as I think the thoughts of God. This *is* the coming up higher.

Years later as I was visiting my mom in the nursing home, Ms. Josephine, a resident, gave me her testimony that bears repeating:

Ms. Josephine sat down beside me and started telling me,

"I have Jesus in my heart. And I know that you do too because I can see your heart." (I was amazed. I knew that her childlike walk was pure and that she really could see my heart.)

She said that one day many years ago she was at her son's elementary school on the playground when suddenly she was at the playground of her elementary school. She saw a long line of people waiting to see a man sitting in the chair and she didn't know why she knew Him, but she knew it was Jesus. She watched as each person in front of her came before Jesus. For some of them, she said, Jesus would hold out His right hand and they would go to the right and walk that way. But for many, Jesus held out His left hand. For those, she said, they would fall on their knees or on their faces crying, weeping and yelling, "Nooooooo!" Finally, it was her turn and she was standing before Jesus. He asked for her name and she gave it. He told her, "Hold on a minute and let me check." He turned around to a pedestal that sat beside Him that held a book. He had a pencil in His hand and said, "I don't see your name in the book." She asked if He would add her name to the book and so He wrote her name in the book. Immediately He was gone and all the people that stood in line, and she realized she was still standing on the playground with her son.

Ms. Josephine went on to say that ever since that day she has been walking *inside* of Jesus. I replied, "Hmmm. I never thought of it that way." She exclaimed, "Well, He's big! Really, really big! He can be ten million miles over there and still be right here with me. I can just keep on walking, but I just can't walk outside of Jesus because He's so big!" After that she just got up and walked away.

This was a concept I've never heard before and it

has totally changed my perspective of walking with God. I felt so honored and special that God would give me this revelation. Thank you God!

This testimony and revelation blew me away! Now I could understand that God wants us inside of Him. There is an inside-ness of God that He desires. We can do anything when we think the thoughts of God. He wants us to come up higher. That's what He's been teaching me for years.

This I know, we can know the thoughts of God, experience the mind of God, climb higher inside of Him, we can share the thoughts of God, and we can listen to His thoughts. We can go inside of God and into His mind. We can come up higher in our thoughts. When we do, we can do the works of the Father because His thoughts are working in and through us! You see God doesn't just want us to know that He thinks about us, but He wants us to know what He thinks. Philippians 2:5 says, *"Let this mind be in you which was also in Christ Jesus..."* So what is this mind that was in Christ Jesus? It is God's thoughts. We are to think like our Father!

So how do we know the thoughts of God? What does that look like?

Many times, it's that soft whisper in your head. It can happen when you are praying, but it can happen anytime that we are willing to listen. Many of us have been taught that praying is all about us talking, but actually half of our praying should be learning to listen to what God is saying. We may not have recognized that it was God speaking—or it could be that God said something that we didn't want to hear. Cultivating a listening ear is necessary to learning the thoughts of God. I truly believe that you have experienced the thoughts of God. This is key to walking as a Believer and doing the impossible.

God knows everything and sometimes He shares His thoughts concerning another person. Obviously, we could not contain all of God's thoughts, so He only shares small portions as He chooses. This is when we know things without knowing how we know them, whether it is about us or other people. This is God sharing His thoughts with us concerning

His purpose and plan. Therefore, in reality, we can only give a true word by speaking the thoughts of God. It never has been about a person reading another person's mail, but it is God sharing His thoughts and we are just repeating His thoughts.

Yes, God is a great, mighty, and holy God, but He really does delight in our knowing Him and abiding in Him. The apostle John even recorded how God desires us to abide in Him and Him in us. Jesus said that if we would live inside of God, that His thoughts and Words would be alive inside of us, that we could ask what we will, and it would be done (John 15:7).

I'm telling you that Jesus made it clear in John 14:12 that if we could just believe on Him and His works that we would do the same works as He does and even do greater works. I know this seems farfetched but I believe that God wants to share His thoughts with us so we can be transformed into thinking like Him just as Jesus did. If we could only believe that God is always thinking of us and ever mindful of our every move, we would not find it difficult to become a Believer. We would be for certain that God will show up for us every time.

COMMANDING YOUR THOUGHTS

Knowing God's thoughts and how He functions is important to believing. Sometimes it takes a better understanding of why we don't believe so that we can begin to believe. Only then we can start learning to command our thoughts. Here is a revelation I journaled about Adam and Eve that helped me, and I think that it will help you.

> When Adam and Eve walked in the Garden of Eden, God's thoughts were their thoughts. They were in the fullness of God's image, so they thought what God thought until the day that the devil planted seeds of doubt in their minds by asking the question, "Has God really said?" (Genesis 3:1).
>
> What is not said but fully implied is that Satan delved into their thoughts to change their thought patterns to his. If he could change their thoughts, they would easily conform to his likeness and in his image. God's thoughts are pure and so were Adam and Eve's until their fall. They could have thoughts of their own but would be patterned upon the principles of purity, holiness, peace, joy, or selflessness. The fall of the thought patterns preceded the sin.

Since we have inherited a fallen thought pattern we have to choose to fight against the sinful nature and choose to embrace God's. God's thoughts are not sinful; they are pure and holy. We can choose to take command of our thoughts and not let the sinful fall of thoughts remain in what is designed to be pure and holy.

Getting Thought Patterns Unstuck

Too often our thought patterns get stuck, even with what we think of ourselves. Way too often we allow ourselves to be self-critical because of our failures. But we have been bought with a price, the blood of Jesus Christ, so what God thinks of you is way more than what you think of yourself. He believes in you far more than you believe in yourself. Here is a journal entry of my first attempts at getting my thought pattern unstuck.

> What others think of me and what I think of myself may or may not be true; and it matters little what people think of me or what I think of myself (other than to control my thought patterns.) What really matters is what Jesus thinks of me. He can only think the Truth. If He says I am, then I am. If He says I'm not, then I'm not. No other human knows the whole truth, we only know in part and prophesy in part. So if my thoughts are not truth, only a perception of the truth, then I ask God to change my thought patterns to be only truth. Any other person's thoughts, feelings, or emotions are (for the most part) irrelevant. I want to know who I am. Who God says I am and not who I've been for years. It's time for me to be a mature woman, one who could help others carry their load. I am praying to get there.

Learning to Hold Every Thought Captive

In 2 Corinthians 1:5 the apostle Paul states, *"Casting down imaginations, and every high thing that exalteth itself against the knowledge of God, and bringing into captivity every thought to the obedience of Christ;"* Here we see that the apostle Paul also had to learn to cast down every imagination that wasn't of God, anything that would be prideful, and to bring every thought captive into obedience to Christ. I knew this scripture but putting it into action wasn't something I had learned to do until later in life. One day the Lord gave me this revelation that helped me to do it.

> I was listening to a message being preached about our negative confessions, I came to understand that I cannot be free from negative confessions if there is bitterness, anger, hurt, or unforgiveness in my heart. My heart first has to be uprooted of these suckers. The negative thoughts come, and I find that I am still powerless to refrain from confessing them. I have tried to hold my thoughts captive unto the obedience of Christ but to no avail. But as of today, I had a revelation that changed my thought process about this issue.
>
> As I began praying, I cried out saying, "Jesus please help me! *You* hold my thoughts captive. I release them to you. I don't want to try and hold them anymore. I am powerless to hold them." I have never thought of it this way before. I have always felt hopeless and helpless to be able to change my thought patterns but today I see that I was never to hold them captive—He was. And He is fully capable. He was right there waiting for me to release them and allow Him to clean my heart. This revelation changed my thought process.

If you're like me in that you don't know how to release ungodly thoughts, just cry out to Jesus. Ask Him to take your thoughts captive. This is a learning process to recognize what thoughts need eradicating.

Learning to Not Grow Weary

Another day came that it seemed like a continuation of a long day at work (like a bad day that wouldn't end). It seemed that my unhappiness was because my heart did not want to be where I was, so I was easily agitated. In my mind I was working a continuous overtime. God had already said that it's a new day, yet my mindset had not made the transition. I was warring this out by the spirit and I was seeing some changes happening in me, my mindset, my tones, my thoughts, my health, my family, and more, so all day I commanded my thoughts to believe in my own prayers.

I was trying so hard to not grow weary in commanding my thoughts. Some days I did great and other days not so much. Then one day I called my best friend Sandra and she said to me, "Nina, you know what your problem is? Your problem is that you are letting your thoughts get in the way of God's thoughts." I was like "Hmmmm! Too true!" She did not know what I was going through and it just came straight from her right after I called her, so I knew this was God letting me know not to give up the battle, and to not let my thoughts get in the way of His.

Learning to Govern Thoughts

I'd like to say that the struggle was over—but it was far from over! (Thankfully, when God sees us trying so hard, He will often have pity on us and help us.) One day in my prayer time I heard the Lord say, "Let the past, be the past. Think no more on the lack or on family problems. Give your thoughts to me. I want them. I am about to put up a guard around your mind to keep out those thoughts which hinder. I had to stop some things so your mind could stay on me. Your thoughts will govern how you see me and how you will feel about what you see." God was letting me know what He was doing to help me learn how to govern my thoughts and bring every thought into the obedience of Christ. He is so faithful to us!

God Stretching Me to Think Bigger

As I kept commanding my thoughts, I began to do much better and it seemed I wasn't weary like I was at first. Then God said, "Stretch and you shall be stretched. Come learn of me in a new way. Close your ears to what you already know and open them to the heavens. Ask me to open to you the sounds of heaven. Close your ears to your own thoughts and I will speak to you. I am glad that you are learning to close the doors to the past and embracing the now. Come learn of me. My trumpets will soon sound. Think bigger, think stronger. I am your mighty God. I am stronger than your enemies. I am mightier than any force on earth."

God was letting me know that all this time of learning to conquer my thought patterns was stretching me and that He was stretching me all the more. It was a huge revelation to me when He told me to close my ears to my own thoughts. I had known to govern what my ears heard on the radio, television, or conversations of people. Never had I ever thought about closing my ears to my own negative conversations to myself. He was letting me know that in order to think bigger (like Him) that I had to stop the small talk I was putting out. I am so thankful for this revelation!

Weighing my Thoughts and Dealing with Fears

We all deal with fears. Fears that we cannot make something happen and no one else will do it for us. I have battled my fears many times. Sometimes I win, sometimes I don't. I find that many times our fears are surrounded by our situations that we cannot control. If we don't get a grip on the fears, then faith has no place. I learned some time ago that fear runs from a situation, faith may leave but it's only to run towards something else. In essence, fear runs *from* something; faith runs *to* something.

Often our fears make us try to force a situation to be in our favor, which is basically trying to override God, and make it happen by our own will. We know that it's far better to consult with God, learn to trust Him, and believe that He *will* work all things out for our good. Some years ago I had a situation that I truly wanted to make happen but I felt like I was going in the opposite direction of what God wanted—even though it seemed to be a good thing. Thankfully God saw my error, had mercy on me, and graciously gave me this revelation. Following is how I learned to lay things at His feet and believe Him to answer righteously.

> Today I petitioned God if I should make a demand on someone for a task that I felt should be done. I had been feeling it for a while and wanted to do it but I knew that I needed their agreement. Suddenly, I understood that a thought like this must be weighed in the balances of God. He is the only one that can give the correct answer.
>
> As I closed my eyes and imagined that I was placing this question on the scales, I immediately knew that I feared the submission, and that I feared the answer. (The reason for the fear was because it was a stronghold in my heart.) I realized that the fear had to be dealt with first, so I asked God to help me release it. I took a deep breath and told God that I released permission to Him to arrest this fear and immediately I felt better. I prayed and presented the thought before God, (which was a valid question upon the judgment scales of God), and I sat quietly as I waited for the Lord to weigh it. In all of this, I knew that His weights were just and true, and are measured by His Word. The next thing I understood was that if it was of my own thinking that the scales would be out of balance. If it was a prompting of the Lord, the scales would balance.
>
> I asked God to allow me to see the judgment, the scales of balance, and then I saw they were out of balance. The Lord began talking to me about the weight He used to balance the thought since it didn't weigh the same. The scripture was Isaiah 45:11 where God says concerning the work of my hands command ye me, but concerning

the things of my sons, ask ye me. That's when I realized that by putting a demand on this person was a command that God alone reserved the rights. Otherwise I would be stepping into what God has reserved for Himself because they belong to God. This I knew to be witchcraft by way of manipulation. Furthermore, I came to understand that if I had made this demand, they would have felt like a failure for not seeing and doing it; and I would be assuming a position that wasn't mine to assume.

Although I remained struggling with fears and needed answers, I still felt that this task must be done, or we would not see God's hand move on our behalf. So, I continued to pray and intercede for the correct way to do what needs to be done and to put my fears to rest. While I was praying this revelation came forth. That if I have fears that are un-arrested, I will see no proof of performance, and then if I mix my fears with their fears, my unbelief with their unbelief, then we have just agreed to a failure, and we are destined to stay in bondage.

I then knew that I had to continue warring with this situation by prayer and fasting because only God could give this victory. One thing I do know that the Lord confirmed to me, was that as I begin to change and others see the spiritual gains and financial gains, they also will grow in faith and will never again struggle in this area. I must learn the power of positive confessions and see the proof of performance that is at hand.

Now today I have entered into another realm that broke bondages off of me. I realized that analyzing a situation is good if it is only done in the perspective of God's righteous judgments. That if I judge a situation, without first placing it on His scales, then I am spiritually out of order. Then I become an unrighteous judge and I will be judged to the same measure. This is really silencing the questions in my head and in my heart and is giving me a greater peace.

After this revelation I now continue to learn how to lay my fears and negative thoughts down at God's feet and try not to control God or other people since all souls belong to Him. I am still learning how refrain from making demands upon anyone unless I consult with God first. My part is to pray and believe God that He will rectify any and all situations. In truth, it really set me free from feeling like I was responsible for controlling every situation or responsible for other's actions. How freeing it is when we realize that all we have to do is to control our own thoughts and actions and let God do the rest!

Thoughts are our Governors

Learning to consult with God and controlling our own thoughts is extremely important to our walk with God. So often we are so outwardly focused on what others are doing, that we forget to focus on what we are doing. We also want to know what others are thinking without keeping our own thoughts in place. We are all guilty of this. Being human, we must all work on governing our thoughts. Here is another revelation that I had about what governing our thoughts will do for us.

> Today I prayed once again to have balance—balance in eating right, exercise, leadership, and more. I seem to have a problem keeping the balance once I get it. My weight is out of control. So I asked God to change the way I think. What I think controls my eating habits, drinking water, and exercising. Those things alone will cause me to lose weight. Then I asked God to change the way I think about leadership. If I'm not leading right, then change me.
>
> This spilled over to some other things. My friend,

Stephanie Billings, a vocal teacher, said that when she gets up in the mornings, she has to *think* the thoughts of a higher pitch to save her vocal cords so when she sings, her voice isn't strained. Since then, I have been trying to watch the pitch of my voice as though I were singing all the time because God desires my song in worship to Him. So, I must think higher to train my voice.

After this I saw a host of other things and prayed over them. My thoughts govern the tones of my voice to be harsh or soft. My thoughts govern my attitude if I am a complainer or I am grateful. My thoughts govern my speech and what I say. My thoughts govern what my heart seeds. My thoughts govern my emotions. My thoughts govern my success or failures. My thoughts govern my fears or my faith. My thoughts govern my character and integrity. My thoughts govern my purpose and plans. My thoughts govern whether I walk in the kingdom of God or not. My thoughts govern my tongue.

I also saw that my thoughts govern my breathing habits. My thoughts govern my prayer life and how I pray. My thoughts govern facial expressions and body language. My thoughts govern my overall health. My thoughts govern my relationships.

In essence, our thoughts are the rudders of a ship that governs where we go and how fast we get there. In reality we do walk in this world, yet if we want to enter into the kingdom dimension, we must train our thoughts with kingdom thinking and mindset. It is not mental assent but another dimension.

Never before had I realized that what I thought wasn't being governed the way it was supposed to be. How could I keep balance in all things if my mindset isn't governed? As a Believer it is vital that we understand that an ungoverned mindset is like a ship that wavers. Our thoughts must be governed if we are going to walk in what God has prepared for us. We must at least attempt to be like Adam and Eve before they doubted and fell into sin. The thought life of believing is crucial in having what you are praying for.

Reaching Higher

God wants us to not just learn to command our thoughts to be in alignment, He wants us to reach for a higher level in faith. That step takes governing our thoughts, taking that leap of faith, and believing in what God says. We are all called to walk in a higher level of faith, and we can be frustrated at others or even ourselves when we don't see it manifesting.

One day I was sad that the saints of God didn't seem to be endeavoring to walk by faith. Perhaps they were having a weak moment, a long delay in seeing anything manifest, didn't know how, or perhaps it was just simply the spirit of entitlement operating through them, so in prayer I began to cry out:

> Lord, I have so little money to bless others. Maybe I'm wrong, but even though I speak faith, I don't see them standing with me for the finances to come. I do not hear their faith proclamations, nor do I hear of them interceding and warring for the breakthroughs. I keep on saying words of faith and courage, hope and trust, love or patience, but rarely do any of them respond with me in faith.
>
> I feel like they aren't with me in spirit, like they think I have flaming words and no action. It's like they really don't believe the words that I speak because I cannot meet

all their needs. Sometimes I struggle with giving them a word of faith because they aren't receiving it but I continue to tell myself, this is your assignment from God. Whether they believe it or not, I must continue speaking faith proclamations. Still yet I look for someone to walk beside me and agree with me. We must walk by faith! We can't rely on the world's system for all our needs to be met—God is our provider. God, I cry out for faith walkers!

I want to continue walking, declaring those things that are not as though they be! I don't want the mindset of the world to be a stumbling block to where I need to be. I am trying to stretch my faith. I know it's not much progress, but I am tired of professing doubt then faith—and teetering back and forth. I firmly believe that I should stand on faith on a steady, constant basis. I have done it before and watched it manifest. Now God help me to guard my tongue from negating your promises to me. No matter what I see or what I hear, I desire to choose faith. I know this will be an extreme challenge but I'm tired of backing up or backing away from what is mine. And when I do fail, help me to have a mindset to get back up quickly. Help me not to lose focus on You in the heat of the battle. If I fail, let me continue to proclaim faith until I can have the strength to get up again. I want to be immovable and unstoppable.

This was definitely a defining moment for me. In being discouraged with what I was seeing, I saw myself so clearly. I knew that I needed to move up higher in faith. I knew that I needed to move to a higher place, to believe all the more that God supplies all our needs according to His riches in glory. God used this one moment to help me put some things in place, to reckon with myself. If I could be the example for others to follow, then so be it. I want to be a faith walker myself!

After this, I chose to continue reaching higher so I could come out and stay out of the valley of doubt and unbelief. I began to make faith proclamations by commanding my body. I was telling pain that it cannot go with me and my belly can't be my God. Many things were stated in this proclamation of faith. Later I began repenting for the harsh, sharp tones coming out of my mouth. I noticed that when I changed my confessions and my tones, that I started walking in a higher level of faith.

Then early one morning I was praying and began declaring of myself, "I am a Woman of Faith. I loose myself from the chains of doubt and unbelief. I am free to have faith and walk with faith. I am a citizen of the Kingdom of God and Satan has no rights to keep control. I choose to walk *with* Faith." Sometime back I understood that Faith is like a person that we can walk with. Faith is a like a Word creature and is our feet. Our faith walk becomes our feet of faith as we confess it with our mouths, so I'm praying for our feet of faith to not be lame. Our feet of faith are required to enter and walk in God's kingdom realms.

Entering the Kingdom Dimension

Jesus made it abundantly clear that entering the kingdom is a faith walk. We all enter the kingdom by believing and accepting Him as our personal Lord and Savior (John 3:5). We have to have faith that God is and that He is a rewarder of those who diligently seeking Him (Hebrews 11:6). Yet we have not totally understood how to walk in the kingdom that Jesus brought. One day as I meditated on the Lord, I realized that thinking with the heart of a Believer also included thoughts of the kingdom of God. I began praying that I would think like a kingdom saint when I had this revelation:

> Last night and early this morning I was praying that my focus would be on what God desired. I specifically asked for my thoughts to be kingdom mindedness. I asked Jesus to renew my mind according to His kingdom. What is

before my mind is what I will become. I asked to walk by faith and to be a Believer—*His definition of a Believer.*

After I was up and getting dressed, my mind started thinking negativity and I told the Lord, "I don't want these thoughts, they hold me bound to this earth. I give my thoughts to you. Jesus, take me to the other dimension you promised. Take me to the other side."

That's when I understood why Jesus once told me, "Let's go to the other side." Up until now I didn't know what He was talking about. It was when I started moving to the other side that I stopped being physically tired and started to run by the Spirit. As soon as I got to the other side, I audibly heard the voice of God. So today, my quest has been to think upon the kingdom of God and become a Believer.

This process of confessing a kingdom mindset created a stronger believing in me. Again, because I was learning to govern my thoughts even the more, I felt like I could do the impossible. As always, the enemy wants to tear down any altars of believing to usher in his kingdom of doubt and unbelief in anything God would do for us. So God gave me yet another revelation to share with you:

Kingdom Mindset Sets Me Free

Today I came to understand that when the devil came to tempt me to regret all the losses of my past, the thoughts of the kingdom flooded my mind and my soul. All I could think was, "I'm in the kingdom. There is no past. There is only now. Therefore, there is nothing to regret because I am in the present in the kingdom of God." There was no warfare or energy spent to overcome thoughts. I kept hearing, "In the kingdom there is no past or future; it just is." This set me free!

Furthermore, the thoughts of having to fit inside the mold of another person's plan and purpose did not exist. I kept thinking, "This is my plan that I am living. It was tailor made for me by God to enjoy what I do." I cannot explain it, but again I was set free!

There was no warring about what others wanted or expected of me. There was no warring about fitting in. There was no warring about anything; it just is. There was no jealousy, envying, or strife within. I was just happy being me.

Stepping over into the kingdom mindset is far more liberating than we can imagine. In that dimension, absolutely all things are possible. I knew that the devil would try me again because that's what he does, but governing my mindset is something he cannot control unless I allow him.

Trusting, Commanding, Believing

As I practiced governing my thoughts it became easier. I began to seek God about how to step into the divine miracles and healings. After looking into my journals, I found an entry that trusting God was imperative; and that if I cannot trust God and learn to command, then I will not move forward. So as of tonight, I understand that I if I want to experience the divine miracles and healings then I cannot allow myself to be paralyzed by my doubts. I don't have the luxury of hesitation. Inwardly I am afraid to step out, but now I realize the real danger is staying in doubt. The cost is too great.

Commanding and Taking Authority in the Spirit Realm

I continued on learning to govern and train my thoughts for a kingdom mindset. As I thought about how God wanted me to move into commanding, I knew that this required a huge change in my mindset. I have been on the border of this for a number of years and it seems that I get a grip on it then I get slammed and lose it, so I worked diligently on my mindset. One day, all day long I kept thinking, "Govern your mindset. What you think will be what you believe."

At one point I saw why I needed to keep commanding when I didn't see anything manifesting; because I must establish my authority in the spirit realm so that the demons know that I rule over them. Strangely enough, I didn't seem to be struggling to remember to do this. I even remembered how I was commanding my mornings as Job 38:12 says, but for some reason I quit—and I was even seeing the results of that commanding. I am now praying to know how to command everything as I submit to God; anything from activities, un-expectancies, finances, healing, demons, and any other things that I know to do.

Overcoming and Rejoicing

As I continued seeking God and governing my thoughts, I started discerning when I was slipping back into the old mindset. I realized how God had delivered me from feeling like I needed to find something else in me that made me second guess myself. I began learning that each time I would command my mindset to think positive, like Christ, my mind would shift to praising myself for the good that I have done—and do. Now I am constantly thinking about commanding and am no longer looking for confirmations to be confident in who I am and what I am called to do for Christ. It is truly amazing to see transformation in your own life by God helping you to overcome the negativity of the doubt and fear lifestyle.

One day, all day I was rejoicing, and my spirit was leaping. I kept thinking about the awesome honor of God allowing me to command a thing and it come to pass. I have felt such a joy and anticipation because I know that God is showing up for me! Although I had not seen the fullness of me or my husband's healings, still I command. Some time ago God told me to keep on commanding because I was forming my world. I am not discouraged because I can feel my spirit man soaring when I do it. A baby doesn't just get up and walk, they keep on trying until they get it right; and I know that I am establishing my domain in the spirit realm. I thought about many dreams of commanding, but one in particular was about repairing a castle in kingdom of God because I was one *under* authority.

It is important for us to believe in who we are and whose we are. Once we know who we are the devil is at a huge disadvantage. You may not attain today. You may fail at some things but get back up. I do that too. I repent often, I forgive myself, and I decide to let yesterday's failures not govern today's victories. I believe in you—but God believes in you more! You can learn to command your thoughts, your days, your mindsets, and your world because you are a child of the Most High God. He has given you this awesome privilege as His child to reach higher. You can do this! You are *Blessed To Believe!*

Realms of New Dimensions

God walks and talks in all realms and dimensions—and He is the Master of them all. Jesus promised us that God has made a place for us, but for now, we know that we are seated in Christ in heavenly places. We could even say that we are seated in heavenly realms (Ephesians 2:6). It is important for us to know that we were designed by God to enter into the realms as it was promised to the church for the purposes of ruling over powers and principalities with wisdom (Ephesians 3:10). In order to accomplish this, becoming a Believer is first. After that, God must prepare us by taking us through a learning process of walking with Him in the deeper things. He is the only One that knows the way there and gives us the power to enter in and do what He says we can do.

Some years ago, God began revealing to me that we are spirit beings more than we are human beings. God is a Spirit and He created us to worship Him in spirit and in truth. Our flesh will die in the end, but our spirit and soul will live on. Whereas our fleshly man naturally resists God, our spirit man naturally longs for God's presence and to walk with Him.

At some point, I realized that if I am going to walk with God, I needed to walk by the Spirit; that God always communes with man Spirit-to-spirit, not Spirit to flesh. If I'm going to walk and commune with Him, I must learn how to walk by the Spirit.

After this revelation, there were other revelations that came forth that helped me to know how to walk by the Spirit into the deeper things. Following are three lengthy journal entries that I have chosen to keep intact because my journal says it better than I can repeat.

God Walks in Full Faith

God is faithful. His being faithful is more than consistency or constant-ness. It is a "Fullness of Faith." God is always walking by faith. He never has a time when He does otherwise. He has no fleshly nature that requires Him to *see* something before acting.

The Bible says that God's voice walked with Adam and Eve (Genesis 3:8). It also walked in the wilderness with Moses (Leviticus 26:12; Deuteronomy 23:14). God's voice spoke into the earth upon His creation and His voice is still walking here. God's voice then is His *feet of faith*.

The voice that walks is the fullness of faith. In Acts 6:8 Stephen tapped into this as did other men of the Word of God. There is a fullness that God is trying to impart to us, but it requires an emptying of ourselves. God's faith still walks in the earth; it never stops nor can it. It is on an assignment to fulfill the Word He spoke (which is always by faith) and it cannot return to God until it completes the assignment. He is the Faith-Full God or the Full Faith God. We are made in His image and were designed, as Adam and Eve were, to walk by faith.

God once told me last year that He could not talk doubt and unbelief, and that the only thing He could speak was faith. Then He said the moment that I spoke doubt and unbelief that we couldn't walk together in spirit because, how could two walk together unless they agree?

(Amos 3:3). Furthermore, we could not commune in the spirit like He desires. That if I wanted to walk with Him that I would have to speak only faith and belief.

God is constantly and consistently only full of faith and there is no doubt or unbelief in Him. Hence, when we profess faith our voice becomes our feet of faith. What we speak in faith is set in motion like thunder rolling through the mountains, and it will come to pass unless we negate by doubt and unbelief.

God requires all of us to walk by faith. Without faith we cannot understand Him, what He does, and what we can believe for.

After God gave me this revelation, He took me deeper still. Following is the second lengthy revelation that again I have chosen to keep intact. These revelations came while I was in worship service at my local church. By this you will see that God longs for us to know the deeper things that we have right at our fingertips if we can only believe.

Spirit to Spirit, Faith to Faith

I was in deep worship at church when I had several experiences and revelations. First, I understood that the new dimensions are new realms. Then God took me to the Realm of Love. It is like a paradise all its own. It is an eternal place. A beautiful place that is tangible in the spirit realm that you can walk around in. It is a garden full of flowers, beauty, and wonders—and at the same time, it has no boundaries. It could take eternity to discover the Realm of Love. I knew that if I had to teach it, I could not fathom its depth or its height enough to cover this vast and endless realm.

Then God shifted me and showed me the Realm of Faith, which, like the Realm of Love was filled with wonder and excitement. It too was a glorious place. You could walk anywhere and as far as you wanted to go, yet it too was endless. And I knew that I was only seeing two realms in this new dimension.

When you are in the spirit realm your understanding is accelerated and you know way more than you would ever know in the natural. So as I remained in the spirit, I came to understand that God not only communes Spirit-to-spirit with man, it goes so much deeper than that. God communes with man in faith-to-faith. He is a God of wonders and creating is what He does—all by faith. When we operate in faith, true faith, then God is capable of speaking to us more. His talk is *not* of doubt and unbelief; He does not, and cannot operate, in that realm. We, as fallen humans, function here but God cannot speak to us as He would love because He can't speak like that. When He speaks, it happens. So He allows us to keep falling until we learn to walk by faith.

I also knew that this faith-to-faith, Spirit-to-spirit is one thing that God is after. Here is what the earth groans for (Romans 8:22). It is the manifestations of us as His sons and daughters. Faith is actually like a key for our spirit to join with God's Spirit.

Then I saw more on faith. Faith is more than a realm, a territory, or a dimension in and of itself. Faith is the transportation in heaven and in the earth; but more, it transports heaven to earth and earth to heaven. Faith then is required to come before God and to carry out our missions for Him. Faith can also be seen as a chariot of God that takes us where we need to go. Now I understand that this chariot I have been seeing is a Chariot of Faith.

Then I saw that faith in us *is* the image of God. When we become the exact replica of God, we are reflected in His eyes, then we can reflect Him in the world. The reflection of us in His eyes means that we see "eye-to-eye" and that's when we become the "apple of His eye." When we are in His image, and in His likeness; we are a reflection of who He is, and the world should see Him, not us.

I also saw that faith then is the very source of life. It is the "light" in the body. It also causes a beacon of light within. One day I watched this movie of a lady that was full of hope and faith for the healing of her son. Her husband wanted her to give up her faith, but she refused, until one day she decided to no longer have faith. Her countenance radically changed; you could even see it in the movie. I had never noticed the countenance change of a person having faith versus unbelief. It was like she was full of life within, then became a dead person. It is now that I believe that faith, and even hope, is the life within us, and without it there is no life. It has done something to me spiritually to see this movie and I am more determined than ever to live a life of pure hope and faith. To believe when there is no apparent reason for believing exists. To keep on hoping in any situation—otherwise I am a dead corpse walking around.

Then I saw how my learning to do so much with so little money is training ground to walking by faith. Jesus had two fish and five loaves and fed five thousand. I'm trying to understand how to defy the laws of earth to usher in the laws of the kingdom into my situation.

Then God took me still yet deeper. Following is the third lengthy revelation:

A Three-fold Chord: Spirit-to-Spirit; Faith-to-Faith; Will-to-Will

I have taught for a long time that we commune with God Spirit-to-spirit. God is a Spirit and we must worship Him in spirit and in truth. But recently, I saw the faith-to-faith and how God cannot speak doubt and unbelief. And if we are speaking those things, we are breaking our communion with Him. So, another depth is to talk and walk faith so we can hear God and see Him manifest to us.

As of the last week or so, I saw another depth. This one is our will. When our fleshly will dies and we function by God's will, our will adapts to His will. I saw a vison (and even felt it as it was happening) that my will and God's will were being interfaced, intertwined, knitted together, whichever that it may be called. This is equally as powerful as faith. When we come into an agreement with the Father's will, our will is made holy. The power of agreement with another human yields a great success. How much more of being in total agreement, total unity, with the Father? We must learn His will, come into an agreement with His will. Then I believe we will see great and marvelous things happening when our will is the same as the Father's.

The next thing I saw was a three-fold chord. When we commune Spirit-to-spirit, faith-to-faith, will-to-will, the enemy will not be able to sift us as wheat like He has done before. Even this week I see that when I talk faith confessions, I am happier, I am joyful, I feel in control of my thoughts and emotions. Plus, I don't feel frustrated because I cannot make something happen. I don't feel anxious because I feel "I can't, and God won't." I don't feel victimized, but I feel like a victor. I don't feel helpless or useless. I don't feel like I'm being used and then thrown away. My confidence in who I am begins to grow more. I feel like my shoulders are back and I am walking upright, with my chin up, and I feel that I can make a difference. I can actually feel myself growing. The opposite happens when I talk doubt and unbelief, and do not come into alignment with the Father's will.

Even though I speak these things and I don't see immediate results, I'm good. I feel better and healthier. I continue on confessing who I am in Christ and how He's made me worthy. This confession also gives me strength in my inward man. It builds my self-esteem, and it also affects my worship very deeply. Worship is based on how well we know God and believing that He is, and does, as the Word speaks.

Recently, I spoke doubt and unbelief, and right after that moment I was flooded with feelings of sadness, like I was a failure. I felt there was no hope for the situation. Furthermore, I compounded this doubt and unbelief by speaking it to another person. This person agreed with me and the weight of doubt and unbelief fell upon me. I wasn't speaking over my situation the Word of God. I then had to return to my prayer closet to get any sort of relief from the weight of it.

What I have now realized, is that faith keeps Satan at bay. Faith is the shield that the apostle Paul spoke of. It shields you from the blasts of more negative words that curse our situations. Furthermore, I also realized that my words of doubt and unbelief were seeds. And as soon as I had sowed them in another person, sprouts came up immediately in them. So then not only was I faced with overcoming my own sins of doubt and unbelief, but I had to battle with them in the other person. I had to cast down those bad seeds that I had planted into them. How can they grow in faith if I am planting bad seeds of doubt and unbelief in them?

I also understood what Jesus said to Peter. Jesus told Peter that Satan was coming to test him, but that He had prayed that Peter's faith would not fail but that Peter would overcome (Luke 22:31-32). What I didn't know until now was that I had always thought it was Peter's sin—and yes, this is partly true. However, Jesus was speaking of faith. Like matter in the natural, so is matter in the spirit realm. If faith is absent, there is not just empty space, something *will* fill it. Doubt and unbelief will replace the faith.

The Bible says that without faith it is impossible to please God (Hebrews 11:6). It is necessary that we believe in order to receive Him or His rewards. Whatever we don't believe, Satan can steal from us and we will have no defense. One time I had a dream that the enemy was attacking me, but as I spoke the Word of God, a fence formed between me and the enemy. He could no longer touch me. I did not altogether understand the dream until now. Once I began speaking faith by the Word of God, Satan could no longer take what belonged to me.

We must get to the place that it matters little what our natural eyes see or our natural ears hear. What matters is what we know by the Spirit. I can "see what I see" but if it doesn't match with what "I know" by the Spirit, I speak against it and say, "I see what I see, but I know what I know, and God has said… about this situation."

As I said earlier, God told me to speak to things—and expect it to happen. He told me not to get tired of speaking to things and quit if I didn't see anything happening. He said that speaking it would grow my faith and confidence and eventually my faith would get stronger. I have started doing this most of the time but sometimes I still fail at it.

I have learned that when I fail, I must get back up in a hurry or Satan comes hard at me. Yet this event of failure becomes a valuable tool of learning. I have learned that failures are just events and are not meant to be for a lifetime. I have learned that "I" opened the door for Satan to torment me when I spoke this evil of doubt and unbelief. It was my own fault for opening the door to Satan's turf. So, I wept bitterly and repented to my Daddy God and asked Him to help my unbelief in where I am so lacking.

Having faith is so much more than just believing for a house or a car. It is a vital part of 1) keeping out of Satan's domain of doubt and unbelief; 2) a source of protection; and 3) a close communing with God such as we have not seen yet, although we are getting there.

I do feel that I am a better person by confessing faith. It is a new life and I love believing God with all that I can and am able. Help me Lord to believe more. All things are possible to those who believe!

What an awesome privilege that we have to mix our faith with God's faith, our spirit with His Spirit, our will with His own divine will! I feel that you will begin to walk into the glorious unknown; into a life that is filled with wonder and excitement. You have been chosen to live in an era of time where the fullness of the knowledge of God is coming forth. A time in history that the prophets of old desired to live in and the angels of God also desired to look upon (Matthew 13:17; 1 Peter 1:12). But you were chosen to walk in all that God has given to mankind!

As I have meditated on these things and upon this particular book, I began praying and the following is more revelations that came forth. And I believe God that gave me these revelations for you, His bride, to learn how to rule and reign with Him. The earth is groaning for the manifestations of the sons and daughters of God. You are definitely privileged!

Following is a portion of the prayer for this book and the revelations that poured forth for His bride:

As I was in prayer about *Blessed To Believe*, I realized several things. First Jesus said that He only did what He saw His Father doing (John 5:19). All this time I saw God at a distance doing something and when Jesus saw it, He moved to be where God was to accomplish it, but that is not what happened. Jesus said in John 10:30 that He and His Father are one. What was actually happening was Jesus was literally *inside* of God; that when God moved and acted, Jesus was there as the embodiment of that movement and action.

When we learn to live inside of God, we won't function under the principles of this world. Just as Jesus defied the laws of nature through raising the dead, walking through the crowds without being seen (another dimension) and many other things He did by God's hand, we also can walk in it.

I feel like this revelation came because what I am to experience and write about is more than having the manifestation gift of healings and miracles. It appears that there is another area like a dimension that has been hid from us all these years of being a true Believer. Stepping into being a Believer will shape the core of these last day's saints. I pray to get to the place where God can envelope me, permeate me, and consume me that I may walk inside of Him, and see His hand super-imposed over everything that I do. Truly this book is about to change me! I am blessed to be a Believer!

Stepping Into Freedom

We can know all these wonderful things, but we must move into action. We must allow the Holy Spirit to take us beyond what the norm of what believing means. Many times, the Lord has spoken to me to not be regimented but to flow with the Holy Spirit. I truly wanted to move by the Holy Spirit and to believe more, yet I was in a pattern of letting Him use me only when I was in certain places at certain times instead of moving when the Holy Spirit prompted me.

As I lay praying about this, I recalled a dream of the Holy Spirit trying to build a tunnel through me. I wanted the tunnel, so He kept on trying to drill it through me. It was like a pile driving machine, but He couldn't break through because I was stopping it. Yet I didn't know what to do to allow it to happen, or make it happen. Finally, one day I quit stressing over Him not being able to do the work in me. I just relaxed and said, "Well, anyway it will happen when it will happen." That's when the Holy Ghost came again to me as I was relaxed and instantly the tunnel happened with no effort at all on His part. Now there was a complete tunnel built through me from top to bottom. From that day on the Holy Spirit flowed freely through me.

Although I knew of this dream, and I knew that the Holy Spirit didn't want me to be regimented, I was still unable to let it all happen in the natural part of me. I received what God wanted to happen, yet I couldn't seem to get there.

I began practicing no regimented prayer times. I totally understand that it is great to have the same prayer time, but I had gotten stuck letting that be the only intentional time of praying. It was the only time of day that I shut down everything to have my time with God. I would feel Him tugging at me to have an impromptu worship time, but I had things to do so I didn't obey. Thankfully He kept coming to me, prompting me when He needed to flow. Now I fully know that He can do more work in thirty seconds than we can do in a lifetime if we will let Him move through us when it's the right time. Timing is everything. God doesn't work by time, but we do, so He must do the impossibilities by His eternal realm, and then usher it into our time.

Still yet in knowing all of this, I find myself continually walking a regimented Christian walk. But if all I am going to do is stay in the same old routine and never venture out to move when God moves, then I'll not step into the realm of impossibilities to make them possible in the natural.

There is another point I need to make that hopefully will help you know where we are and how we can miss moving into the impossibilities.

> Some time ago I had another dream where all Christians were in a prison. We were happy and satisfied. The compound was actually a very luxurious place. The sleeping house had hundreds of twin beds, but all was clean and well organized. We could go swim, learn how to snorkel, play tennis, or any other fun activity. We were treated like we were very important. We were well fed and well taken care of, yet we were still in a prison compound. No Christian wanted to leave this safe haven where we had everything that we needed without having to pay for anything. It was like being on vacation all the time. The problem was that we were incarcerated, we were in prison, and we liked it and had no plans to leave. I, myself, hadn't

realized that there was more outside of the prison.

But one day I saw this high lookout tower to my right with a prison guard keeping watch, and on my left was a small mountain. He was making sure no one ever left this compound. As I kept looking I saw four men that were dressed like cave men and I could tell they were ancient. They had walked through the compound, walked directly in front of me and around to the right side of this small mountain. To my surprise there was a small gate just large enough for one man to pass through at a time. This gate was overrun by weeds but would open. The problem was that the mountain was in the way of the gate opening. These four cave men saw me watching them, but they never spoke to me, they just talked among themselves then looked up at this small mountain and said something. I don't know if I couldn't understand what they were saying because it wasn't loud or because I didn't know their language. But then, right after they gently spoke, the mountain began to move. As the ancient mountain moved, I noticed that it had a face. There were two indentions for the eyes, a rock formation for his nose, and a slit in the rocks for his mouth. This ancient rock mountain groaned like an old person that had joint problems. He had not moved in so long that it pained him to move and I felt sorry for his pain. The rock mountain moved in a clockwise motion only for a short way then he stopped. Those four ancient cave men looked at each other, looked up at me, then opened the gate and left. Outside of this prison camp was a forest, so as soon as they went through the gate, they disappeared quickly.

No one else saw what I saw or heard what I heard. The guard on the tower never saw or heard it either. I knew to not whisper a word about what I saw. Many days went by without anyone but me knowing. Then one day the guard picked up his binoculars and noticed that the mountain had been moved and the gate was left open. He then sounded the alarm. That's when everything changed for all of us. The militant guards shut down all of our playful activities and from then on we were treated like slaves. The militia was sent out to find those who had escaped the prison and we were no longer given luxuries of any sort. Yet I still did not have any understanding why those four cave men wanted to leave such a wonderful place of beauty and luxury at no cost to us. And I would often wonder what was out there. I questioned in my heart, "What is out there? Why did they want to leave? How could they so easily speak to a mountain and it move?" All that I knew was to keep my mouth silent and tell no one of what I had witnessed.

After I awoke this morning the Lord reminded me of these two dreams, and I understood that they went together. I came to realize the importance of these two dreams and how they play a part in the life of a Believer. We often don't realize that we are allowing ourselves to stay incarcerated in our doubt and unbelief. It seems that we are comfortable in what we know. We believe that it's normal to not believe. People seem to be happy living a life that's less than what it was intended to be.

Yes, for us to escape the land of doubt and unbelief, we will surely alarm the kingdom of darkness to go after us. They will even retaliate on those we love and to punish them because we are choosing to break out. But God is mightier, and we can speak to the mountains and watch them move—but first we must be a Believer.

Notice that these four cave men (whom I feel were four angels that went to the four corners of the earth) never shouted at the mountain, they never got excited, and never caused a scene. They knew their authority and walked in it. They were quiet and were sure of themselves. Even when we break free, we must guard against getting into a regimen of doing the same old things all the time. When we do realize where we are as opposed to where we are capable of going, we will realize that we are falling way short of where we could be. We must follow the leading of the Holy Spirit.

Now I know that God was revealing to me that I had gotten comfortable, but God was showing me where I was. I was supposed to follow those cave men out of the gate, but I didn't know I was supposed to. Today I'm still praying to follow those that God has sent to show me the way to becoming a true Believer, to walk in faith that will move the mountains. You too can choose to walk out and allow the Holy Spirit to use you. Only then will we walk into the realms of the impossibilities. We can do this!

Go Higher, Go Deeper

I firmly believe that your eyes of understanding have been opened to a whole new level of believing. And now you know how to walk as a Believer like you've never known before. No matter who you are or your age, you are all called to be a Believer.

Believing in God and communing with Him is the gateway to walking in the glory realms. Believing is necessary to walking in the kingdom dimensions that He has promised you. Luke 17:21 says that the kingdom is within you, but you must learn to believe from your heart in order to activate what God has already imparted to you. Your believing is a powerful tool. Even if no one else believed in the mighty working power of Jesus and His blood but you, you alone could convince the world that Jesus was sent of the Father (John 17:20-22).

As stated, Jesus' work was to cause all people to believe in God thereby reconciling them back to God, but they had to first believe before they could be reconciled (John 6:29). Just like God sent Jesus into the world so that they would believe in Him, so you too have been sent into this world to demonstrate the manifested glory of God through healings, miracles, signs, and wonders. Therefore, believing is *your* works too. You are God's ambassador sent into the earth to train people to believe in God. Not just for salvation, but also to walk as a Believer, believing that they can do all things through Jesus Christ (2 Corinthians 5:18, 20; Mark 16:15-18). It is your works to teach and train people to walk as Believers and advance the Kingdom of God on earth.

In every dispensation of time, people have needed demonstrations of signs, wonders, healings, and miracles for them to believe in Jesus and what He does. It's true that people really do need the outward signs to convince them of God's power and readiness to interact with them. It's not just about God's power to save and heal them, but for them to believe that God truly loves them and has their interest at heart. Even when they claim they are a Believer, frequent reinforcing of believing is necessary to cancel negativity, doubt, and unbelief. You will know they have become Believers when you see their child-like faith where they don't try to rationalize, analyze, or use logic, they simply believe at face value what God says. The Bible says that except we believe as a child, we cannot enter the kingdom (Matthew 19:14; Luke 18:16-17; Mark 10:14-15).

Always remember that believing Jesus for healing, miracles, or any other manifestations is a matter of the heart. You were born into the eternal kingdom from your heart, and thus, your belief system abides from within your heart. People in heaven are already living in the manifested kingdom, but here on earth, you can only see the kingdom manifesting as it comes out of you. You must believe it from your heart for the kingdom to be activated and the miraculous to come forth.

Remember to guard your heart since Satan's job is to steal and/or destroy your belief system. He will try to get you to walk with God by your intellect. He wants you to remain operating by the world's system rather than by the kingdom principles. He wants to keep you from walking in the kingdom dimensions and seeing the healings and miracles manifesting. But be wise and remember that you walk by believing God and not by what you see.

Remember that God is never far away, and it is His pleasure to work His will through you. Because you live inside of God and He lives inside of you, you know perfectly well that He is for real. When He's that real to you, everything is believable, everything seems possible because He is right here within you, ready to perform the miraculous. As Mark 11:24 says that when prayer is coupled with believing we will have what we request, then these signs must follow because we are Believers (Mark 16:17). You are a Believer.

Once you truly know that God can and will do all that He said He would do, and that you can do what God says you can do, nothing will stop you from moving forward. With confidence you will leap out, knowing that God will back up His Word. Jesus is always present with His Believers because this is still His works. Mark 16:20 says, *"And they went forth, and preached everywhere, the Lord working with them, and confirming the word with signs following. Amen."* Even though Jesus was ascended into heaven, Mark noted that Jesus was working with them to making Believers in God and He will do the same for you.

So I ask you, "Now do you believe? Now will you accept that you are called by God to be a Believer?" If you can, all things are possible to you. The kingdom is already in you and all you must do is believe in your heart that you can do the impossible.

I encourage you to conquer your fears within, release your own negative thoughts of doubt and unbelief to God, and learn to govern your thoughts until your thoughts conform to God's. Learn to speak in faith even when you continually don't see anything happening. Learn to commune with God Spirit-to-sprit, faith-to-faith, and will-to-will. You were a Believer when you were saved, now remain in that realm of believing. You belong to the Father. You were created to walk in the realm of believing with Him. You were, and are, created to walk in the Realm of Faith, into the Realm of Love, or to be seated with Christ in heavenly places. The Father believes in you more than you believe in yourself. He loves your faith confessions and He absolutely loves to commune with you.

Of course, you will have battles, but God created you to be more than a conqueror. Let's confess it, "You are a Believer." You already believe in miracles and you believe that all things are possible with God. You know that God has answered many of your prayers. You have already begun taking the next steps to believe in what you couldn't believe for as you read this book. You desire the greater things. I encourage you to continue denying the power of unbelief and doubt in your life. No one—absolutely no one possesses the ability to make you stop believing in God and His miracles. You alone possess that power.

I believe in you too. I have prayed for you, that you will be able to grab ahold of the awesome privilege of believing with a child-like faith. I pray that you will exceed your own expectations in believing.

Remember you are *Blessed To Believe*, and you have the privilege of going on to higher realms. So, go higher, go deeper, and believe that you will do the impossible—and you will!

ABOUT THE AUTHOR

Dr. Nina Gardner, C.Psy., Ph.D,. and Th.D., author of *Worship that Touches the Heart of God* and *Lester the Scared Little Leaf*, (both also available in Spanish), has other self-published works. She has written college curriculum for theology, ministry, Christian counseling, prophetic, and apostolic courses and especially loves writing about worship and the persons of the Godhead.

She and her husband, Milton "Bobby" Gardner, Jr., served many years in churches and held many different positions. In 2002 they were ordained and birthed One Voice International Ministry. Together they teach and train ministers as well as do marital conferences and revivals. Dr. Nina has a radio broadcast *In His Presence* on Buenas Nuevas—Memphis 105.5 FM and is founder of *Voice of the Prophetic School* in Memphis, Tennessee and Troy, Missouri.

For more information, visit our website at www/onevoiceint.com or contact Dr. Nina at onevoiceint@gmail.com for speaking engagements.

To order more copies of

Order online at:

- www.CertaPublishing/Bookstore
- or call 1-855-77-CERTA

Also available on Amazon.com

Additional Books by Dr. Nina Gardner

Worship THAT TOUCHES THE Heart OF God

Available in both English and Spanish versions.

Order online at:
- www.CertaPublishing/Bookstore
- or call 1-855-77-CERTA

Also available on Amazon.com

Additional Books by Dr. Nina Gardner

Available in both English and Spanish versions.

Order online at:
- www.CertaPublishing/Bookstore
- or call 1-855-77-CERTA